Spir...
Jean-P...

Jean-Pierre de .... was born in 1675, probably in Toulouse, and took his final vows as a member of the Society of Jesus in 1708. In 1731 he was appointed spiritual director in charge of the Jesuit retreat house in Nancy, where he undertook the spiritual direction of the Nuns of the Visitation. In 1740 he returned to Toulouse and remained there until his death in 1751.

Kitty Muggeridge was born in Switzerland in 1903, was educated at Bedales and has travelled widely, first with her parents and then with her husband, the journalist Malcolm Muggeridge, whom she married in 1927. Sher has translated La Fontaine's Fables from the French (Collins), has collaborated with the late Ruth Adam on a life of her aunt, Beatrice Webb, and has translated Jean-Pierre de Caussade's treatise on Self-Abandonment to Divine Providence in *The Sacrament of the Present Moment* (Fount).

Spiritual Letters of Jean-Pierre de Caussade

Translated by
KITTY MUGGERIDGE

from Lettres Spirituelles of
Jean-Pierre de Caussade
presented by Michel Olphe-Galliard S.J.

Collins
FOUNT PAPERBACKS

First published in France as *Lettres Spirituelles*
Desclée de Brouwer in 1900
© Desclée de Brouwer 1900

This translation first published by
Fount Paperbacks, London, 1986

Made and printed in Great Britain by
William Collins Sons & Co. Ltd, Glasgow

Contents

Foreword

Jean-Pierre de Caussade was born on 6th March 1675, no one knows where for certain, but it may have been in Toulouse. The earliest mention of his name is on 16th April 1695 when he was admitted into the noviciate at Toulouse. This anonymity is in keeping with such a passionate advocacy of self-abandonment. In 1704, after studying theology at the university, he joined the Jesuits and became a priest. From 1698 he spent a number of years teaching, from college to college, a variety of subjects which included Greek, science, philosophy, metaphysics and the humanities. He left his career as a professor, which he did not like, in 1678 and found his true vocation when he was appointed spiritual director to the sisters in the convent of the Visitation Order in Nancy. It is in this convent that God gave him the opportunity to broaden his knowledge of souls and develop his own spiritaul doctrine.

The central theme of de Caussade's spirtual teaching is abandonment of self and the act of submission to the will of God. It is the remedy he prescribed for all the afflictions and suffering of which the sisters complained in their letters to him. He was much loved by them, and one of them wrote that he was "the person who takes the place of God for me on earth and is responsible for my conscience".

The similarity of this doctrine to that of the Quietists, about which controversy was at its height among the clergy at that time, is said to have been the cause of his being relieved of his duties at the convent and sent to teach in various theological colleges. In the chapter on "Disgrace", it is clear from his letters of reply to the sister that he found his duties and this theological colleagues uncongenial. Nevertheless he submitted to the trials and tribulations of his circumstances, in accordance with his teaching. When finally he was able to return to the convent and resume his directorship of souls and the life of meditation which he loved, he was joyfully welcomed by one and all.

It is clear from these letters that it is a mistake to suppose that by abandoning the world for the religious life in a convent we can escape from the vexations and sufferings of our mortal existence. In a convent they are inward, spiritual and of the soul. In the world they are outward, temporal and of the mind. They may be different in kind, but they are there in both places.

In conclusion it must be admitted that de Caussade's doctrine of self-abandonment to Divine Providence, and his view that suffering is not only to be endured but welcomed as the will of God, who loves and knows what is good for us, presents a valuable and hopeful alternative to the prevailing doctrine of "self-fulfilment", and contains a powerful message for today's material society, which sees suffering as totally unacceptable.

Suffering is the condition of our existence on earth.

1

Peace Within

My dear sister and beloved daughter in God,
The peace of Jesus Christ be always with you.

1. I thank God for all the noble sentiments He continues to inspire in you. While you maintain that determination to devote yourself solely to God in complete and total submission to His good pleasure, fearing neither dryness, darkness, temptation nor indifference, all will turn out to your greatest spiritual advantage.

2. Your dread of being mistaken about the peace you experience in the midst of inner suffering is quite unnecessary. I can see from what you tell me that, although you don't realize it, this is true peace. It is the foundation of everything and a great mercy which you must try to preserve, cost what it may. Every attack and wile of the devil is aimed at making you lose, weaken or destroy it; but stand fast in faith and trust, and beware of pledging yourself to any vow, whatever it may be.

3. The total seperation of body from soul is a great advantage which leads inevitably to perfect love and Divine union.

4. Your secret foreboding of approaching death can come from either God or the devil. If this foreboding increases your detachment from everything without worry, despair or doubt, it comes from God and must be preserved. If not, it must be dismissed since everything that comes from God has good results, and it is by them that souls can be identified. All the repugnance you tell me you feel is intended to detach you from all human support in order to have no other than God's; your religious observation of this is excellent. But I am surprised you have not yet learnt that when God allows darkness every good sentiment vanishes, like the sun at night. There is nothing to be done except to remain resolute and at peace, while awaiting the return of the sun and the arrival of day when all will be as it was.

I allow you to write to me once, twice, three and four times a year and whenever you judge it necessary. If I agree, I will be very prompt to reply.

*

The sister did not hesitate to use the permission given to her by her director, separated from her as a result of a circumstance which must have been particularly painful to both of them. The following letter shows us something of the anguish his departure caused his pupil.

LETTER 2

My dear Sister,

I am neither cross nor surprised by your great distress at

the departure of your director. If, rather than allowing yourself to be disheartened by this, you can overcome it, it will give place to the most excellent submission to God. In this way, little by little, you will detach yourself from the world, and unite yourself to Him who is your sovereign good. Oh what good fortune, what assurance for the next life, what unfailing peace in this one to belong to God alone; to have no other treasure, support, help or hope than God! I wish I could send you the beautiful letter one of your sisters sent me recently on this subject. For one month, she tells me, this one thought – "God alone, I have nothing but God alone" – consoled and sustained her so firmly that instead of regret she experienced an inexplicable fund of peace and joy. It seemed to her that God had taken the place of her director, and He alone would henceforth instruct and correct her.

It is also to Him alone that I recommended you when I left and which I continue to do now. Here is Mother Superior's [Mme Rangfaing] farewell on the eve of my departure: "Father, I say farewell to you in the love of God." That same evening she comforted all the other sisters and the following day resumed her normal routine.

LETTER 3

Your great longing is excellent. But you must always be sure that it is under control and resigned and consequently peaceful since as you know well, our noblest desires are a mingling of nature, and passion when they become violent, restless, impatient and unruly. It is also in order gradually to purify our most saintly desires that God often delays so long in granting them, since the impatient requests of nature are not worth granting. Only desires inspired by the Holy Spirit, always gentle, patient and quiet, are worthy of being listened to and fulfilled by God. As far as you can, remain calm and even at peace in holy joy, in order so to experience all the wellbeing which fills a contented and joyful heart.

LETTER 4

You are worrying yourself about me while I myself am thinking quite differently. I bless God each day for that happy stroke of Providence by which I learned to die to many things in order to live in God alone. I was not so buried alive at Nancy. Many things inwardly and outwardly sustained me and made me feel that I was alive. None of that just now. It is as if I were in a real desert, alone with only God. Oh! how delighful that is. It is a dying to everything bodily and even spiritual, a kind of annihilation which must be passed through in order to be restored to a new life in Jesus Christ. A life entirely in God, detached from everything, stripped of every possible gratification in which the senses could play a part. God wishes me dead and detached from everything in order to live only for Him. His holy will be done in everything and for ever! That is the firm pillar to which we must remain immovably attached. That is the sure and unshakeable foundation of all perfection.

When God sends us some heavy crosses and we sincerely wish to endure them bravely for the love of Him, He never fails to give us invisible support, so that our resignation and inner peace always matches the weight of our cross and sometimes exceeds it. Such is the love of Jesus Christ our master, and the power of inward grace with which He has favoured us. From this we conclude that for our part, as far as serving God and our spiritual advancement are concerned, everything depends almost entirely on our good will. God mercifully does the rest, well knowing just how frail, wanting and impotent is our capacity for good. He supports and strengthens us, working through His Holy Spirit.

The practice of accepting every minute the present situation in which God places us, alone can keep peace always in our heart and benefit us without hurry, worry or agitation. Furthermore this is very simple and we should cling to it firmly and resolutely, resigning ourselves to whatever else regarding it God may wish.

The clearest indication that we are not mistaken about the love of God is:

1. When we wish everything that happens will please Him.
2. When we can suffer without a murmur in order to please Him.
3. When we have a great horror of sin, even of the most trivial kind, and do our best not to commit any consciously.

Neither resentment nor a tendency to suffer inwardly are in any way signs of lack of obedience but only of human nature and consciousness of our sacrifice. Do nothing against God's command, say not a word of complaint, of self-pity. This is perfect obedience inspired by pure and perfect love. Ah! if under similar circumstances you knew neither to do nor say anything, but to remain in the inner silence, humbly silent in respect, faith, adoration, obedience, abandon and sacrifice! This is the great secret which will sanctify all your sufferings and even greatly soften them. We need to practise this and conform to it little by little, never worrying or despairing when we fail, but returning at once to that great silence, untroubled and humble. It is true that I did not find my sudden loneliness here all entirely agreeable at first, but soon I accepted it with my heart and soul. I love to leave things to Providence. That is my great aim, to follow it blindly, regardless of everything: of place, work, time and, in fact, of everything. I am delighted that your very eagerness itself serves to moderate your desire, and, as you say, to remind you of many ways which bring God on your side, and so to speak of winning His heart.

Since God graciously allows you so generous a taste of our cherished principles of obedience, abandon and sacrifice, you may be assured that He makes you do and practise them partly, at least, inadequately. But since you are so enthusiastic about everything, you wish in this respect to reach the height of perfection all at once. This is not impossible. You must advance little by little, even committing minor sins which humble us and make us recognize our great frailty before God. Inward revolt against these circumstances does not rule out obedience in the higher regions of the soul. Read and re-read chapter fifty-seven of St Francis de Sales book, addressed to a nun of the Visitation Order called Marie. This letter has always enchanted me. It will put at your fingertips the difference between the two wills of the soul, the knowledge of which is indespensable for the life within.

LETTER 5

It is not necessary to remind me to pray to God for you. It is something I take care not to forget, especially since I know you to be in a state very painful to nature; although all the more beneficial. I will admit, however, that it has never occurred to me to ask God for anything for you other than patience, obedience and resignation to all His holy will and abandonment to His merciful Providence. This is because I am strongly convinced of God's great mercy to you, and the need you have for it, a need all the greater because you yourself are unaware of it. When this storm has passed, you will understand two things clearly and distinctly. You will not know how to show your gratitude to God for having been willing, Himself, to undertake the task of bringing about in you, in a few months, what with His usual help you would only have been able to achieve in twenty years, and to purge you by these bitter potions of certain traces of self-esteem, very hidden, and pride, all the more dangerous because it is subtle and scarcely noticeable.

From these poisonous roots arise an infinite number of imperfections of which you are scarcely aware: futile qualms of conscience, still more futile complaisance, useless worries, unprofitable longings, vain and frivolous hopes, false suspicion of your neighbour, jeering at others, and arrogant behaviour. Without suspecting it, you run a grave risk of long remaining a prey to every fault, full of vanity and self-confidence, without ever being able, or wishing, to sound the deep abyss of your perverse and corrupt nature. It is this depth of misery which God makes you feel today. Not in every detail, because if you saw it in that light it would scarcely touch you; but broadly speaking, and in general. This accumulation of imperfections is like a heavy burden. Do not search for some great sin hidden in your conscience. What is really the matter is even more terrifying. It is that chaos of inward misery, failure, and minor continual and almost imperceptible faults resulting from the pride we have been speaking of. God is doing you a great favour by making you see this in His light. Without it you never would, not even by its effects. In this respect you were as blind and indifferent as vicious men are with respect to glaring faults, of which the force of habit conceals their gravity. You were equally ignorant of that leaven of corruption in yourself which spoiled and poisoned all you did, even the things you did with good intentions.

And so the celestial phsician has greatly favoured you. His severe treatment of your sickness opens your eyes to the internal absesses which are destroying you. The sight of that filth pouring from them filled you with a healthy disgust. In fact, neither self-esteem nor pride could hold out against such a humiliating and distressing sight. I conclude from this merciful design that you must neither wish nor hope that the treatment to which you have been subjected should cease before a complete cure has come about. Until then you must be prepared to recieve many a cut from the lancet, to swallow many a bitter pill. But continue always to keep your courage and fill your heart with childlike trust in the charitable and fatherly hand held out to you. Humble yourself under that almighty hand. Annihilate yourself continually. Let it do what it will. Never depart from the contempt and disgust of yourself. Think only of your faithlessness and ingratitude. Look at yourself, not in the false mirror of your self-esteem, but in the mirror which God holds up before your eyes to show you as you are. From this constant view of yourself will come forgetfulness of self; humanity and admiration for others. "Come and see", says the Holy Spirit, that is to say, approach the Lord, and in the new light He shines on you, look on what you were, what you are and on what you would have infallibly become.

Be sure never to abandon prayer or Holy Communion, for in these lie your strength and protection! As for sins, you will not commit any, or at any rate no serious ones, as long as you are afraid of displeasing God, as indeed you are. This fear alone will reassure you. It is a gift from the same hand that invisibly supports you in your trials.

We must be patient. Solace will come in time and will be lasting . . . whereas trials are soon over. But pitiful human nature cannot tolerate suffering and is impatient to see it depart. The important thing is to gather the fruits of the cross. Let us pray, then, and cry out for the strength we do not possess ourselves. This is a fundamental truth which you will only discover through your own experience. This is why God prolongs it until you are so saturated that it leaves an impression that can never be obliterated from your soul. You speak of perfect love. Know that souls have never found it without experiencing torments within. It is therefore essential that the longing for this blissful outcome should make you welcome the torments. This alone can lead you to it. The more you do so the sooner you will see their end, and the more fruitful will be the result.

March bravely on your way, then. Rejoice every time you discover a fresh failing. Sigh for the happy moment when the mere knowledge of that abyss of misery will destroy all your confidence and self-satisfaction. It is then, fleeing with horror from that rotting tomb, that you will enter with transports of delight into the bosom of God. It is after having thus completely cast off self that we come to think only of God; to depend on and rejoice only in God. This is the new life in Jesus Christ. This is the new man born after the death of the old man. Hurry then, to die, like the silkworm, in order to become a delightful butterfly that flies in the sky instead of crawling on earth, as you have done until this day.

I received your letter, my dear sister, on the great day of St Michael, the day for which I have a great love because of these words: *Quid ut Deus*, which is my motto. I have no other consolation than those words, although as you know, for a long time they have been for me, by God's order, nothing but affliction. I certainly have walked alone on my way, having the saints in mind, in continual criticism from friends around me and darkness and doubt within me. This way was obscured by God, who led me along that narrow, dangerous path, as in the dream I had the other night. Thinking to descend from a height along a path going across the mountain side, the slope became so steep and the path so narrow that there was room only for my feet. Dreaming, I soldiered on, clinging to the hillside, until, at last, I reached a broad path of solid rock, whereupon I awoke.

Since those of whom you speak are not as impatient for my return as you are, neither are they so eager and prompt to respond. God will interpret as He pleases the lively encouragement you bring to so many people and especially lately to M... What delights me in this is that your enthusiasm serves to curb your impatience and to remind you of many ways of pleasing God. I think this will make

His enterprise successful. God be praised in advance, whatever the outcome.

My dear girl, allow me to say that although I see in you changes which please me, and which God hides from your own eyes, it seems to me that you are not yet quite reasonable on the subject of our great project.

1. You will easily understand, as I do, that the people of whom you speak, having at this point neither your eyes nor your heart, your thoughts nor your sentiments, it is natural that they do not have the same enthusiasm. Rather, I am surprised that many of them, through petty motives and contrary views, have not put obstacles in your way.

2. You must realize that for the most part, when all hope is lost, it is then we should be most hopeful. Because then, by putting all our trust in God alone, we engage Him to take a hand in the work. And everything succeeds when God wills it to, because He knows how to use the difficulties and obstacles in the way of mankind for His own purposes. Believe me, if it is to our advantage then do nothing — the work will succeed. If it were to our disadvantage, could God do better than to impede it?

As for what you are hoping for: await patiently a successful outcome. It is in the hands of Providence, to whom therefore you must submit with the most humble obedience possible to you. To be honest, I am delighted to be able to foresee all the difficulties. It is the will of God, who has brought it all about. Furthermore, I have never doubted that every difficulty you mention, and perhaps many others which you do not yet see, are, as M.D. says, in order to test you in particular so that, if you hold firm to the resolve you have taken, this delicate matter will be a source of infinite satisfaction, strength and encouragement to you in the future. Never doubt it. Never allow yourself the least word of resentment or bitterness against anyone who does not hold the same views as you do.

I have no further details for you about my health, unless it be that God preserves it and graciously uses it all; not only uses it, but even allows me to lose it in the service of His glory alone, since He is all and we are nothing. All is due to Him and nothing to nothingness. I am delighted by the good intentions of the Provincial, since God wishes it to be so. But it seems to me that, on the whole, you look too much to human beings. As far as I am concerned, thanks to God, I look always to Him and depend only on Him and, for the love of Him, on certain men. It is He who inspires and directs us. I wish to receive nothing but from His hand; to be obliged only to Him; to be grateful only to Him, and to find favour only in Him; and to know that, as regards the present moment, it is, in fact, Divine Providence who arranges everything in a unique way. If you only realized, as I do, how little men contribute to it. And how they misconstrue everything! But above all God knows how to bring about circumstances and carry them out as He pleases. May he be for ever blessed for the various arrangements of His Providence, which are as supremely wise as they are beneficial and advantageous to His poor creatures.

Why still all these imaginary fears, so soon to become a memory? I don't see the least sign of them, and here we take no account of them, on the contrary, quite the opposite. Why worry in advance about something that may never happen? Sufficient to each day is the evil thereof. These anxious forebodings have distressed you in the past. Why surrender yourself to them?

LETTER 6

Sufficient to each day is the evil thereof. Everything that happens is ordered by Divine Providence. So let us remain humble and obedient in every event, great or small, to all that God wishes or allows. Oh! how blind we are when we wish for anything except for what God wishes! He alone knows the future and everything that is going to happen. I am firmly convinced that we should all be lost if God granted our own wishes. That is why, said St Augustine, God, in mercy and compassion for our blindness, does not grant us what we desire and ask for. Often he gives us the very opposite as being in the end the best for us. Truly, it seems to me that we in the world are like poor invalids who, in a frenzy of delirium, beg for precisely that which will bring about their death. Their requests are refused in pure charity and for the best intentions. O, my God! If this truth were once recognized what delightful obedience, what total abandonment of self to God's will and to His Divine Providence would we have? What peace of mind and heart in everything and for everything! I say the same about the various aspects of the soul. Since even when it is our own fault, God has so willed it and we must submit, let us detest our sin and accept the painful and humiliating consequence, said Francis de Sales! Oh, if this were once well understood, how this would abolish the useless trouble and worry so destructive to the peace within us and to our spiritual progress.

Will I never be able, with the help of grace, to introduce into your soul, and especially into your heart, that great precept of faith so tender, so consoling, so loving and so peaceful? O, my God, we should repeatedly tell ourselves that all your holy wishes should be accomplished in us but never our own. Yours, because You can never wish for anything but the best for Your creatures if they submit to Your wishes and never to their own, which are always blind and usually mistaken and pernicious. If ever, O my God, through ignorance or wilfulness I should have any wish other than Yours, may I always be confounded and punished, not on account of Your justice but on account of Your pity and Your great mercy.

Come what may, said Francis de Sales, Jesus lives. I will always side with Divine Providence, even though the worldly-wise may tear their hair in anger. When the light of heaven shines upon us we see things very differently. What a source of peace do we not discover in this way of thinking and seeing everything. O, how happy saints are! O, how peacefully they live! And how miserable, blind and senseless are we not to accustom ourselves to think as they do; to prefer to exist buried in the sombre gloom of that hateful worldly wisdom which makes us unhappy, blind and sinful! Let it be our aim, our care and our intention to conform to God's holy will in spite of the rebellion within us, which God in His mercy allows, in order to accustom us always to obey Him in everything, giving up everything in silent adoration, submission and love with confident abandonment.

LETTER 7

I pity you for the continuation of your cross. But I would pity you much more if you did not know how to profit from it, at least if only by virtue of necessity. Remember our essential assumptions:

Firstly that there is nothing so insignificant or apparently so negligible which is not ordained by God, down to the fall of the leaf from a tree! Secondly that God is wise enough, good enough, powerful enough and merciful enough to turn the seemingly most unpromising events to the advantage of those who know how to adore and humbly accept and cherish His glorious freedom.

Is there anything more consoling as far as faith is concerned? When once we have truly understood that a natural rejection and aversion, far from hindering the benefits of obedience, only augments them if is for the most part sincere. And when we recognize, moreover, that a little impatience and some minor disappointments of which we are scarcely aware, are imperfections and fragile faults which do not destroy our submission but only spoils it a little. Often they are necessary in order to maintain our humility, without which all would be ruined and lost through our vain complacence. Do you remember M. de Cambrai's great saying? "To be able to suffer is God's great mercy, not heroically or with great courage, but modestly and humbly, sincerely. That is how we learn patience and humility at the same time."

As for the great suffering you tell me of, add it to your other cross as though it was an extra weight allowed by Divine Providence and, instead of one *Fiat!* say two. Then rest in peace in your inmost soul which, helped by grace, can remain resting on the surface untroubled in the midst of storms and tempest. It is like being at the foot of those high mountains, where it rains and freezes, whereas at the summit we can enjoy clear skies. Always remain, then, up on those serene heights in order to escape the lightning and other alarming accidents.

It seems to me that you are still too concerned about

your morality. As for myself, thanks to God, I only wish to see Him, so as to depend on Him alone and for love of Him and those who are crucifying us. It is He who allows and influences our actions. I wish for nothing except it be from His hand; to be obliged to no one but Him; to offer thanksgiving for everything to Him always.

If you knew, as I do, how little men contribute to what happens you would realize that Divine Providence manages everything in a unique way and arranges it all for the best. God knows how to provide for the circumstances and essential needs that best please Him. May He be glorified for and in all things for ever!

I realize that my behaviour is considered a little too simple. But never mind. I find that holy simplicity which the world abhors so charming that I would not think of correcting it. Everyone has their ways. I respect the prudent and the wise, but I am content to be one of the poor, the humble and the meek of whom Jesus Christ speaks, and after Him, Francis de Sales.

We may be quite sure that God arranges everything for the best. Our anxiety, our unrest and our impatience often make us imagine obstacles when there are none. Let us follow step by step the arrangements of Divine Providence and we shall discover what is required of us: and that will be what we want ourselves. We shall want for nothing else. O how much better God knows what is good for us than we do, blind wretches that we are! Very often our misfortunes and our sufferings come from the fulfilment of our wishes. Let us leave everything to God and all will be well. Abandoning ourselves totally to Him is the only way well and truly to promote our real interests. I say "real" because there are many false ones which lead to our ruin.

My abandonment to Divine Providence, as I conceive it,

is not as heroic or difficult as you think. It is the basis of perfect peace. In it we discover unfailing repose even in the most distressing events. How richly we are rewarded for the trifling and pitiful sacrifices we make to God! Having made them we make no more, because there is nothing else we wish for. We no longer wish for anything ourselves, but only for what our supreme Master wills for us and according to His divine bounty. O what joy in this world and the next!

The presence of the celestial doctor, as of the earthly one, is excellent when available. But when Divine Providence deprives us of it we must learn to do without it. We must put all our trust in God alone, who is the great All and a very precious addition to anything we lack either spiritually or bodily. Whoever relies on anything else will often find himself easily distressed.

LETTER 8B

I pity your frailty, but at the same time congratulate you, because it is well known, although seldom recognized, that patience and long-suffering bring us closer to God than does taking action. It is on the cross of Jesus Christ that our Redeemer, our Advocate and our beloved Lord, has saved us.

Since you occasionally see N... do speak to him especially of the need to stick to a regular rule of life and daily regime so as not to be governed by whims, moods, illusions or chance. Speak to him of the need for inner contemplation so as not to be at the mercy of foolish thoughts and futile hopes. Speak to him of the need always to submit to Divine Providence in whatever situation he may find himself, whether it be spiritual or temporal, or whatever the cause, even if it is a result of his own doing. Speak to him of his need to resist his wilfulness, his irritation, his eagerness and impatience, even in the most trifling incident. Speak to him again of how to overcome his indifference, his contempt, his intolerance, his disappointment and his own nature in the most blessed circumstances. Tell him never to fear or lose courage on account of sins but humbly to turn immediately to God, not in vexation, regret or disappointment, but with sweet, gentle, unhurried and confident trust. Finally, speak to him of the need to cherish that most precious spiritual treasure which is inner calm and peace of the soul, that comes from obeying the bountiful and holy Will of God in confidence and submission to His fatherly Providence united in Jesus Christ, to His example and the example of those who become saints by conforming to it.

LETTER 8A

You would like to know, you say, the time of my return. The fact is that I don't know it myself, and I neither can nor want to. I surrender and abandon myself entirely to Divine Providence from one day to the next. You do the same as far as you are able. There's nothing better. It is only in total obedience that we are able to find and experience an unfailing peace within. The greatest good fortune for the next life is to die to everything in this one. Happy is he who, by his daily death, prepares for the true death through which we enter the true life.

Likewise, let us abandon ourselves to every wish of God, and we shall soon be relieved of our burden. Then we shall see that in order to make progress in the paths of salvation and perfection, there is, in the end, little to be done. Without worrying about the past or the future, we must look to God in trust, as to a Loving Father who leads us by the hand through the present moment.

I do not yet know what my future is to be, and I am very relieved. This total ignorance leaves me completely submitted to Divine Providence where I am utterly at peace and in my element, without a care, like a little child sleeping gently on its tender mother's bosom, wanting all and wanting nothing, that is to say, everything that God wills and nothing He does not.

In this happy abandonment I discover peace and a profound repose of heart and spirit, which frees me from a thousand vain thoughts, hundreds of disquieting ambitions, and of all care for the future.

Every condition, place and task through which God has led me, has been a mixture of so much good and so much bad that, if I had to pass through them again I would be unable to choose between them myself. Can we do better, then, than to leave everything to Him to decide for us? Besides, we have only one great and important aim in this world, eternal salvation. Provided this essential aim is achieved all is done. The rest matters little!

LETTER 9

I can clearly see from your letter, my dear sister, that through all your inner ordeals and perplexities you have made solid progress.

1. To recognize the value of the inner life and peace of heart, and to strive for them in the face of every

discouragement, is already a great deal. The rest will follow in its own time and will be the fruit of your compassion towards others and yourself. We must accustom ourselves to accept everything at the hand of Divine Providence, and to bless it in all and for all things. If we accept all its provisions in this way what gives us most distress will become our greatest blessing. Let us trust in God, and never be defiant. Let us always be prepared to make sacrifices to Him if need be, and in this way we shall always receive fresh favours and by them lay up treasures in heaven.

2. Evil thoughts and feelings about our neighbours, if they are not given way to inwardly or expressed outwardly, are not sinful, but rather to our credit. Be steadfast in charity, and little by little they will vanish and all will be well. Should one or two inward or outward evil reflections slip from you, first be ready to humble yourself before God, untroubled and in peace, and then repair as generously as you can the pain you may have caused or the reputations you may have damaged. You will gain more by this atonement than you would have lost by your sin.

3. Your dryness and indifference when receiving the sacraments are certainly a very great affliction. Endure it humbly and patiently. Do what you can, quietly and in perfect faith. It is the severest penalty God can inflict on a soul in order to cure it of introspection and the indulgence of self-esteem.

4. Try, during the day, to make everything an occasion to lift up your heart to God, effortlessly and unhurried. Observe the most filial obedience to all the various

provisions of Divine Providence. You will gain more by that alone than from any spiritual exercises of your own choice and liking. Above all, let your perfection consist of wishing precisely for what pleases God, and how it will please Him. His pleasure is, after all, the basis of all good will and the principle of all perfection, whether on earth or in heaven.

LETTER 10

I admit that a visible guide is a great support and mercy from God when it is of the kind that is needed. But if, when Divine Providence reveals none, or removes it, we know how to say with all our heart: "My God, I have nothing but You!" What we gain by that would be worth more than all we could gain from our directors. I assure you that God often removes all human support in order to gain all our trust Himself. O, if only we knew how to give it all to Him without sharing one little bit of it with whoever it might be! How richly rewarded we would be for the lack of human help! What peace, what inner freedom would we not experience! But this, like everything else, will come gradually by means of sacrifice and self-abandon. We only have to wait patiently on God in order to enrich ourselves with the gift of grace. But this costs dear to those who are eager and impulsive.

You are quite right to feel easy about your general confession. But you say "sincere confession". That is where it is so difficult to comfort good souls, especially those of your sex. You must know, I repeat, that a truly good repentance is hardly ever conscious. God does not wish it to be conscious, so that He can keep us in awe and completely at His mercy. "But," you repeat, "it is God who has done it all, has taken it out of my hands, and I have not been able to sacrifice anything myself." And that is precisely what I find the best and greatest conclusion for you because it is a definite sign of His divine favour. I find that this is how He always acts in respect to most of His chosen souls, and by which He keeps them inwardly humble with feelings of deepest gratitude.

For the rest, what you call stupidity and callousness is precisely God's gift to you. Would to His goodness that you were still more foolish and indifferent about everything in this world! That is one of the principal ways in which grace operates in us when God wishes to win over and take total possession of a soul, to belong to Him for good.

LETTER 11

1. You say that at present you have no help. My God, you are indeed to be pitied to long so much for trifling outward support! These are excellent when God grants them, but when He removes them, ah how much better it is then to depend on Him alone, and to be able to say a hundred times over: "Lord, You are my all, but You suffice me and I await nothing except from You." The almighty hand of God then comes to take the place of that feeble broken reed.

2. You complain that you can only take advice under compulsion.

And I tell you that after so much advice and so many letters you should be in a position to advise others. Then, after having lifted up your heart to God, what is there to do but to take, there and then, the course that seems most convenient and consistent with virtue and God's will? Then what comes of it pleases God. Then we have done well and could not have done better under the circumstances. Do you imagine that God asks the impossible of you? He loves honesty and simplicity, and He is satisfied when we do what we can and the best we can, after having trustingly asked for His divine guidance.

3. You are unable to foresee anything that will not cause you suffering and affliction. Oh, God's merciful bounty which must have brought about, or will bring about, as essential, your total detachment from all creation! Is it not to His most cherished soul that God is so gracious? O, daughter of little faith, but well beloved of God, complain after that if you dare! You still insist that God alone can know what you are suffering. If you do not insist too much I congratulate you with all my heart. It is how the blessed mother St Teresa spoke during her great spiritual trials.

4. It is a good sign when we find life sad and bitter. But death is frightening because of God's judgement. However, provided this fear is not overwhelming, it comes from the Holy Spirit. I would be anxious for all who are without that holy fear.

LETTER 12

My dear Sister,
Can't you understand once and for all that everything

succeeds if it is God's will, because He knows how to use the difficulties themselves and the objections men raise for their own purposes? Believe me, if it is to your advantage it will succeed whatever anyone does. If, on the other hand, it is not to your advantage, can God do better than prevent it? And so it is God alone who foresees the future and all its consequences. As for us, we are blind wretches who always anticipate dangers of every kind, even in events which appear to us in the most favourable light. Can we do better, then, than to leave everything in God's hands? Can our future be safer than in the all-powerful hands of that adorable Master, that good and gentle Father, who loves us more than we love ourselves? Where shall we find a surer refuge than in the motherly bosom of that loving Divine Providence? That is the blissful home where our heart must come to rest. Apart from that there is no true resting place or peace . . . only ambition, trouble, resentment and distress in this life and threats to our eternal salvation.

LETTER 13

Peace in the heart, trust in and obedience to God with a longing to unite ourselves with Jesus Christ, that is the best and most useful preparation for the Eucharist. But the devil tries to sidetrack us. He stops at nothing that might disturb our peace because he knows very well that if this divine peace were once well established in the soul, nothing would trouble us. Everything would fly, so to speak, along the highway to perfection. So let us not be put off for no matter what special reasons. Let us turn humbly to God, trustingly, and without guile, as St Francis de Sales says, with the upright heart of one who sincerely seeks Him.

As for praying, you know very well what I have so often recommended. You have only to allow your inner meditations, and the lifting up of your heart to God during the day, to become so frequent that this can, when necessary, take the place of prayers, without, however, ceasing to pray as often as you can.

Above all, read the letters of St Francis de Sales. You will find some of them so in keeping with the state of your mind at present that you should read them as though that great saint had written them for you from heaven above, and that the Holy Spirit had dictated them to him for you.

You wish to know what I ask God especially for you. It is this, it is all so easy that this alone will charm you.

1. Outward restraint which little by little will subdue your passions. That is to say, speak mildly, without exaggeration or fervour as though you were of a phlegmatic disposition.

2. Inward tolerance of yourself and others, especially of servants and those near to you. Do not on any account, allow any outward sign that might contradict this virtue to escape you. Or, at any rate, repair it and obliterate it as soon as possible.

3. For the successful outcome of all things, total abandonment to Divine Providence without excepting your own progress in virtue, wanting only as much of it as God wants so that you can say "I want what God wills".

4. Peace within your heart which is never troubled, neither by your mistakes nor by your sins, which will make you turn to God with calm and gentle humility as

though you had not had the misfortune to offend His divine mercy, or that you were certain of His pardon. Simply follow this advice and you will see how God will help you.

LETTER 14

Despair is one of the most dangerous temptations. Have a little more trust in God. Be sure that He will accomplish the work He has begun in you. Your unnecessary apprehensions for the future come from the devil. Think only of the present, leave the future to Providence. It is the good use of the present which will assure the future. Try to attach yourself and conform to each and every wish of God down to the smallest detail. Therein lies all virtue and all perfection.

For the rest, God allows our daily sins in order to humble us. If you know how to enjoy the fruits of this experience and to remain calm and trustful, you will find yourself more fortunate than he who rarely commits any. This flatters his pride and fills him with foolish self-satisfaction. How admirable is God's wisdom. He knows how to use our sins themselves to our great advantage. We must hate them and calmly take pains to overcome them.

In your work submit to God, but without bustle or impatience. Just do your best at what you think is your duty and then leave all the rest to Providence, without a care or anxiety, so as to have as far as possible a free spirit and a quiet heart. You will remain at peace in the midst of difficulties and confusion by conforming to the merciful and indulgent will of God. May He be blessed in all and for all, now and for ever.

LETTER 15

Everything which moderates the impatience of your desires and holds and keeps them in suspense is God's special mercy. Try, therefore, without effort to profit by it so as not to allow free access into your soul of anything such as ambition, fear, hope, sorrow, joy or wilful despondency. In this way, little by little, the peace of God will find its way to the bottom of your heart. The less conscious it is the more precious it will be since it can only come from God.

When we no longer care or are able to engage in an active life we experience a delightful solitude all around us. Nevertheless the difficulties and annoyances of Divine Providence are preferable. It is true that the first of these is sweeter and more consoling, but the other, being more painful, is also more beneficial when it is God's will to confront us with the choice. From which I conclude that there are many ways of coming to God. Each one of us must follow his own way without envying others, or wishing to be other than what God wishes. In that alone consists all our joy in the present with the hope of eternal bliss. For at any rate, our will to believe that everything comes from God, to which we must also submit, we must always suspect our enthusiasm, especially for good works. We must patiently suffer what God suffers. Having done what we reasonably think we can and should do in the light of God, let us remain calm and untroubled in obedience to all His adorable wishes.

I begin by telling you that I always find you too eager and impatient about the date of my return. When we have obtained what we long for, three months earlier or later are not worth worrying about.

Two things console me about your suffering. One is that the result of your great distress over the separation which I have always seen, as far as you are concerned, as God's test is so beneficial to your salvation that in itself is has served you better than my presence would have done. You will not understand this, but I have, and you must take my word for it. The necessary delay in my return will also benefit you even more for the same reason. Let us have patience.

LETTER 16

"God has left man to judge for himself. Life or death; good or evil are before him. Whichever he chooses will be granted him." In these words the Scriptures make us understand that man is free, and that salvation depends on the good use of his freedom. It is true that since original sin freedom for good is weakened and, on the other hand, greatly fortified for evil. But with the help of grace, which never deserts him, it is always in his power to strengthen freedom for good which is naturally very weak, and to weaken freedom for evil which is unfortunately too strong.

There are three kinds of good which our feeble freedom achieved with great pain and much difficulty:

1. The good essential for salvation, the omission of which is a mortal sin.

2. The good necessary for less fundamental reasons, the omission of which would be a venial sin.
3. The perfect good which we neglect at great risk to our hopes.

Every impulse which weakens our resolve to fulfil our essential duties – hatred, desire for vengeance, anger, undesirable relationships, avarice, envy, etc. – is also the cause of our spiritual ruin. The same applies to inclinations which lead to venial sin and wilful wrong doing, since those who neglect trifling sins will gradually succumb to great ones, says the Holy Spirit, and if we are slack about one single point in the pursuit of perfection we shall never reach it.

But also every victory which strengthens our will for good is the main-stay of predestination and salvation.

And so our continual aim must be ceaselessly to fortify our frail freedom for good and to conquer our inclination for evil. We have three means of assuring and hastening the success of this resolve. The first is to make generous sacrifices to God by valiantly overcoming our reluctance to do what costs us most effort. The second is to make the small daily sacrifices for which there are frequent opportunities, with a strong, generous and all-embracing faith. The third way, the most important, is prayer: a simple and humble prayer inspired by the Holy Spirit, since it is He, said St Paul, who taught us to pray, who suffers us, who prays in us with cries and indescribable groans. The Publican is an excellent example for us. He prayed silently in humble contrition. The greatest and most wicked of sinners can pray like he did. This is how, from the depth of their misery, if they remain faithful, they will raise themselves up by degrees to the most perfect saintliness.

Although the mission has been over for some days, this is the first moment I have had to reply to various letters, and I begin with yours. Despair is one of the most dangerous temptations. Have a little more confidence in God and be sure He will achieve His purpose in you. The Nancy mission will not prevent my seeing you to tell you that I have to stay on till the end of . . . Who knows whether God will not wish me to stay on longer? Your fruitless apprehensions about the future come from the devil again. We must think only of the present and, better still, leave the future to Providence. The good use of the present ensures the future.

2

Carrying the Cross

The disastrous floods you describe are, as you say, an evident manifestation of God's scourge. Happy are those who take advantage of it for the life to come! These scourges willingly accepted from the hand of God are worth more than all the wealth in the world that is soon gone.

These disasters are also a warning for many and, alas, a reproach for others. But is would be their own fault and a very serious one. For what is more reasonable and, so to speak, in a sense easier, than to make a virtue out of necessity? Why steel oneself uselessly and criminally against the paternal hand of God our Father? He only hits us in order to detach us from the worthless goods of this world, attachment to which deprives us of the eternal riches faith promises and which we would lose for ever. On these occasions let us take useful and careful note of this passage by a father of the Church:

Such is the bounty of the Almighty Father of men even His anger comes from His mercifulness, since He only punishes us in order to save us. Like a good surgeon who cuts to the quick the rotting flesh in order to preserve the rest of the body.

Let us accustom ourselves to seeing all things in the wide vista of Faith. Then scarcely anything in this world will touch us. Neither desires nor fears, not even the lively hopes which so often trouble the soul and disturb the peace of our heart and our tranquillity, will make much impression on us.

Oh, what blindness among men! And what obstinate clinging to their opinions! How seldom do we admit that we have failed to listen to or accept good advice! Oh, how right St Francis de Sales was to say that we are full of unreason! At least let us recognize that abyss of misery and blindness into which we have fallen through our sins. Let us humble ourselves unceasingly before God. Let us learn from this to be mistrustful of ourselves and on guard against warped judgements and opinions. St Catherine of Genoa was so obsessed with this that she wanted continually to cry out so that everyone could hear: "Lord, help me, assist me, take pity on me!"

As for our present suffering and those we dread for ourselves and others in the future, a single *Fiat* will suffice to lay up a store of credit in heaven, of peace, and tranquillity on earth, or at least of strength and comfort through all our suffering and fears.

LETTER 18

You must not be surprised that one does not make as much headway inwardly as one does in other undertakings. The work of our sanctification and perfection is lifelong. I note that your natural zeal and eagerness interfere with everything. From this comes the anxiety, despair and agitation which deter you from your purpose, lacerating your heart. Here is the remedy. As long as you truly wish to belong to God, and have the desire and esteem for what will lead you to Him, and the courage to recover from your little failings, you are in a favourable frame of mind in the eyes of God. Have patience, then, learn to tolerate your own frailty and afflictions as you would those of your fellows. Look to God alone and to His Holy will, which most often operates in the depth of our soul without our knowledge.

You talk to me of penitence! Ah, my dear girl, is there a better way, or one in which there is less will of our own, than in patiently enduring every cross which comes directly from God, when they are necessary, inevitable and the natural outcome of the circumstances in which His Divine Providence has allowed us to find ourselves involved. These are the heaviest crosses, but they are also the most sanctifying since they are all the crosses of God, of our Heavenly Father and of Divine Providence, not being of our own choosing, like those we suffer voluntarily and shape for ourselves of our own free will in the place of those which God alone shapes for us as He shapes all our crosses. Leave Him to act. He alone knows what is best for each one of us. Let us be resolute, submissive and humbled before every cross of God. In the end we shall find peace within our souls, since by our acceptance we shall have deserved that God should make us feel that divine unction which has been attached and enclosed in the cross since Jesus Christ died for us.

But the life within? you ask. Ah my dear girl; how many are mistaken about it! The inner life, serene and untroubled such as I have sometimes described to you in order to inspire you with a taste for it, is only to be found in two kinds of people:

1. Those who are completely detached from the world and removed from all its perplexities.
2. Sometimes, though more seldom, those in the world when by virtue of having conquered self and detached themselves from everything, they live in the world as if they were not in it, that is to say, being only of the body and not of the spirit and of the heart.

But isn't there yet another life within which, having none of these comforts, is all the more beneficial? And it is this one to which you must cling, the other may follow. Now this inner life demands two things of us. The first is to accept everything coming from the hand of God: affairs, adversities, sickness, difficulties, annoyance, etc. But what if we escape them sometimes? That will always happen to some extent. We must expect it. What must we do then? You know what you must do. We must humbly recover our serenity and obediently resume tranquillity; quietly humiliate ourselves before God and never lose heart or be discouraged. All this as serenely as possible, being careful, according to St Francis de Sales' doctrine, to guard against distressing yourself about being distressed, aggravating yourself about being aggravated, worrying yourself about being worried. For this is going from bad to worse. Distress within is always increasing. This is a great danger to ardent souls.

The Cross of Sickness

LETTER 19

1. As regards your illness, whatever you may say about it, rest assured that your soul will profit by it as though

from a spiritual cleansing. To suffer peacefully is to suffer well, especially when we do not purposefully make pretentious acts of acceptance. An obedient heart offers them and makes them unconsciously by that humble and willing non-resistance. Moreover, learn to know that suffering a little and modestly, that is to say without feeling heroic as if you were overwhelmed by your misfortune and within an ace of giving up, full of self-pity, giving way to a rebellious nature. Know, I say, that it is a great mercy, because then we suffer humbly in a light-hearted way, instead of feeling very courageous and strong, and very consciously resigned, something which swells the heart with pride. Without realizing it we would then become full of self-confidence, inwardly proud and presumptuous, instead on the contrary of finding oneself small and weak before God, humiliated and ashamed of suffering so feebly. This is a very consoling and definite truth, very hidden, entirely inward and little recognized. Remember this on all occasions, when feeling the agony of the cross and suffering, you also feel your helplessness. Nevertheless, overcome your feelings, remain in peace and quiet, holding on to everything God wills. It is the most blessed way to suffer. It is what M. de Cambrai calls becoming small in one's own eyes and not allowing oneself to be defeated by the feeling of helplessness in suffering. If this truth were generally recognized by people of good intentions, ah, how peacefully and quietly would they suffer, without worrying about self-respect or their helplessness and lack of courage to endure their suffering bravely. Remember all this in your daily affliction from the person in whose care you are, and in your dislike for others.

2. As far as slight encouragements are concerned, it is true that all those people who visit the sick must not be believed. Their flattering talk is, as you say, just a trick; but it is no less true that we must accept humbly, without scruple or question, everything the doctors, the superiors and the nurses order. Often even, apart from obedience, we also find an even greater self-denial, by a definite renouncement of one's own ideas, judgement, wishes, and self-will. This is another truth, the ignorance of which mortifies many devout people, even in their mortification, who are attached to their own ideas, and very opinionated in their supposedly saintly wishes, since our pride and self-will spoil everything, corrupts everything even the most saintly intentions themselves. Oh, he who once and for all renounced all his own devices and desires, how happy and content he would be!

The increase of peace and rest during prayer is God's grace. Hold fast to it and don't worry about any distractions, which, although they distress you, nevertheless may come to you.

3. To return to your meditation when you find yourself drifting away from it, do not try to make it conscious and active; let it be passive. This is deep tranquillity of heart, and freedom within, disengaged from everything in the world without. Then God is less the main object of our thoughts than the principle of life which governs all our actions. It is a certain subtraction during which we are tempted to imagine that we are thinking of nothing, because on one hand we are detached from tangible things while on the other we have only a general idea of God so vague and obscure that it is lost in the soul. Or rather, the soul is lost in it and seems to vanish and escape from itself.

In this state we do, peacefully and without hurry or anxiety, everything we have to do because the Spirit of God gently suggests it, and stops and suspends our action as soon as pride begins to interfere. Then all we have to do is to put aside our activity, in order to calm ourselves and to enter our passive contemplation, which is only that deep peace in the soul of which I have often spoken. In this way you will resume that simple and almost continual prayer, which consists in remaining silent within and putting aside all thoughts rather than fighting those that come and seeking those that don't.

4. The impatience which awakens in you for long periods, tormenting you inwardly, is extremely beneficial. It purifies and humbles you, so that gradually you become like those little children whom Jesus Christ wished us to resemble. You are quite right then to say that we need to have patience, gentleness and sympathy for ourselves, perhaps more than for our fellows, as St Francis de Sales says.

5. Continual changes of mood inwardly are a good sign. It is how the Holy Spirit makes us respond to His intentions. By constantly changing ours we have none of our own and so are ready to take on whatever the divine Spirit wishes, who blows where and how He pleases. It is, says M. de Cambrai, like a continual inward melting down and recasting, which makes the metal pliable and liquid like water which, having neither shape nor form of its own, takes on the shape and form of whatever vessel into which it happens to be put.

6. Never take the least trouble to steer your way through all these different situations. You have only one simple and very easy thing to do. It is to see where the main inclination of your heart leads you, without consulting your mind or your thoughts, which would spoil everything. Always act with that saintly simplicity, good faith and upright heart, never looking back or aside but always ahead only to the present moment, and I will answer for everything. Do you realize that this is a continual death to self, the most complete denial of the ME and the true sacrifice of abandonment to God in the mystery of faith? As for the fear of being abandoned by God, that is a temptation and snare of the devil. Drop all those anxieties and vain fears, as though they were the most wicked thoughts. Never entertain them willingly.

7. You say you never feel the slightest remorse within, either for good or ill, an indifference which seems to you terrible. It is your state of mind. All susceptibility must be banished. That is the condition of perfect faith. Fear nothing, go your way in peace, in simplicity, in total submission without question or regret. When these are needed, God will supply them, or replace them by an inner feeling or an unconscious impulse which will guide you in everything more safely than could all your gloomy reflections, whose loss and deprivation you might perhaps regret a little. Happy are the poor in spirit, for the Kingdom of Heaven is theirs! Love that poverty within you which deprives inwardly, deprives us of ourselves inwardly as outward poverty deprives us of wordly goods. This is how the Kingdom of Heaven is formed within us.

8. If you had been more willing to give in you would have been able to be obedient, loving and eager at the same time, by sacrificing yourself to help with what was expected of you in spite of your antipathy, etc. This would have been even more advantageous to yourself, since what small acts of humanity, patience, restraint, modesty, self-control, vigilance and charity would you not have found occasion to do. But you did not have the courage. At least humble yourself before God and learn now to become little in your own eyes.

9. The advice God wishes to give you through the person in question is a greater favour than you imagine. Here is what you must continually do!

(a) Endure patiently unintentional outbursts and annoyances, as you would a fever or a headache. It is in fact a fever within, frequently recurring. Oh, how agonizing, humiliating and painful this is, and as a result how sanctifying!

(b) Never talk about her as others do, but always kindly, since, after all, there is good in her, and in whom is there no bad? Who is perfect in this world? Perhaps without wishing to or thinking about it, God influences her more through you, than He influences you through her. "God often uses a diamond to polish another diamond", said M. de Cambrai.

(c) When you have committed some fault, quickly recover by meekly humbling yourself without spite either against her or yourself, without vexation, regret or worry. Our faults overcome in this way become profitable and advantageous to us. It is by means of these daily sins that God continually reduces us and keeps our heart truly humble.

10. As for the rest, when all is said and done never interfere with anything unless it is your duty to do so. Neither speak nor think about it, abandoning all to Divine Providence. It matters little if everything should vanish and everything perish, provided we belong to God and will achieve salvation.

11. But, you will say, what will happen to me then? It is this. I don't know and I don't want to know, because I would be very distressed to remove myself from that happy state of submission which enables me to live completely and wholly in dependence on God, to live day by day, hour by hour, moment by moment without bothering myself about the future or about tomorrow. Tomorrow will look after itself. The hand that supports us today will support us by His invisible hand tomorrow. The manna in the desert was only given for the present day: whoever, in defiance or false wisdom gathered up enough for the morrow found it rotten. Let us not, through our ingenuity and our blind and anxious forethought, make provision as faulty as God's is enlightened and reassuring. Let us depend solely on His Fatherly care, surrendering ourselves totally to it for all our earthly, spiritual and eternal hopes.

That is the true and total abandonment which will engage God to take responsibility for everything for the sake of those who surrender everything to Him in order to honour in this way, in spirit and in truth, His almighty kingdom, His wisdom, His power, His goodness, His mercy and all His infinite perfections. Amen, Amen!

LETTER 20

My dear Sister and beloved daughter of our Lord, the peace of Jesus be always with you.

1. I have never spoken to you in the way you mention, but only as to a poor novice whom God in His mercy is putting to the test in order to purify her in preparation for her union with Him. You are inclined at present to dwell on those terrible recollections of having strayed from the path of virtue. You must endure them without protest as long as it pleases God, just as you would those in which there is only delight. This vivid feeling of failure and darkness pleases me, because to me they are a clear sign that the divine light is growing in you, unknown to you, and so creating a deep humility in you. The time will come when the thought of those torments, which today horrify you, will overwhelm you with joy and a delightful tranquillity. It is only when we have arrived at the bottom of the abyss of our nothingness and we are firmly established there that we are able, according to the sacred books, to walk with God in righteousness and truth. Just as false pride removes God's favour from the most deserving soul, so this happy state of deliberate humility and this liking for self-abasement attracts divine grace to the most unhappy soul. So do not look to any other help, either during life or at the hour of death.

It is in this voluntary annihilation that you should have taken refuge in order to escape the dread which assailed you during your last illness. Do not fail to do so if ever Satan tries to catch you in the same trap.

At the approach of our last hour our pride relies on some

tangible sign of moral support for our past actions. We should wish for no other than that of pure faith, and God's mercy and the grace of Jesus Christ. The moment we wish to belong to God alone that is enough to gain that support. This rest is mere vanity.

2. I approve, moreover, of your inward and outward conduct during your illness. I see that God has wisely hidden from you the few good things He has made you do, otherwise they might have been an occasion for a great deal of self-satisfaction and complacency, which would have spoilt everything. I know better than you what took place and I bless God for it. He has held you up in your weakness. Now you have only to thank Him without enquiring whether everything was really supernatural. Leave that to God. Try only to forget yourself in order to think of him.

3. Why should you apologize so much for your melancholy spirit? Let everyone think what they please about the subject. You have only to please God!

You must not willingly give a moment's consideration to what He may allow people to say or think about you. All that only fosters your self-esteem and vanity.

4. I rejoice that you should find peace where you would least expect to. It is the sign that it is God's wish for you, and that He wants you to find peace only in the accomplishment of His Holy will, which is a great mercy. If I have been unable to feel very sorry for you in your last illness it is because I do not consider bodily suffering, which procures great benefits to the soul, a real hardship.

5. You are convinced that you do nothing and deserve nothing. And so there you are, drowned in nothingness. Oh, how fortunate you are, since it is certain that, from the moment we are nothingness, we are in God who is everything! Oh, what a precious state is that state of nothingness! It is necessary to pass through it before we can be filled with God, because we must be entirely empty within before God can fill us with His Holy Spirit. And so what troubles and worries you is the very thing that should calm you and fill you with saintly joy in God.

6. The acceptance of everything in the present and the future, without reserve, is one of the most acceptable sacrifices we can make to God. This regular habit is worth everything else that you could possibly do. And so your one and only task is to adhere continually to all the ordering of Providence, both within and without. Do precisely that, and little by little God will accomplish all the rest in you within. That is a very simple undertaking and all to your interest.

7. I am not too cross about the unfriendly behaviour of your companion. She was not as much to blame as you in what has so greatly aroused your anger. God has allowed it in order to humble you, by making you aware of what you are like when He leaves you to yourself for a while. You must offer this sacrifice to God. Humble yourself obediently and without resentment. Remember what St Francis de Sales says about this.

8. God requires us to fulfil our duty. But he does not ask us to enquire whether it has any merit or not. You think much about yourself, you are too preoccupied with

yourself under the pious pretext of making progress on your way to God. Forget yourself, in order to think only of Him, and submit yourself to the commands of His Divine Providence. It is then that He Himself will help you, comfort you, and lift you up when and as much as He pleases. What have we to do then but to please Him, and to wish what He wishes in everything and everywhere? We seek perfection far and wide, and yet we almost hold it in our hands. It is to wish for what God wills in everything and never for what we will. But to arrive there we must renounce and sacrifice, so to speak, all our most cherished interests, and that is what we do not want to do. We would like God to sanctify and perfect us according to our ideas. What wretchedness, what pitiful blindness!

LETTER 21

I always urge you to be ever patient and abandoned to God because you always need to be. Since God alone is everything the rest is nothing, so let us hold on to Him closely, firmly and unshakeably. He has His ideas and intentions which He has not allowed us to fathom. There is no other remedy for all our ills, no other comfort in all our suffering, than to surrender to the total abandonment through which we shall deserve that eternal fortune, that true and everlasting life.

Endure your rebuffs and infirmities as though they were an extra purgatory through which we all have to pass in this world or the next. A simple "Thy Will Be Done" in all your suffering within and without, will sanctify you in the eyes of God. Remember the great saying of St Francis de Sales to one of his penitents: "My dear girl, repeat throughout the day, Yes, heavenly Father, yes, always yes." That is a very short and simple way to perfection, and yet in that consists all perfection which we so often go a long way to find when it could so easily be found within our own hearts without searching outside it.

I am delighted and edified by your noble and saintly reflections. With regard to the little consolation you get from your fellow creatures and your idea that it is a punishment for your too great tenderness and excessive compassion for your parents and your friends, that is God's merciful gift to lead your heart back to Him alone, for whom we are uniquely made and without whom we could never find true peace.

I continue to notice that your spiritual desolation comes from having no spiritual support within. I have often told you, and I repeat again, that this support is a gift from God. But with respect to certain people, I contend that the lack of it is, in the end, a greater blessing which contributes more than anything else to sanctification. Listen to me without prejudice. When God honours a soul by being jealous of her heart, the greatest favour He can show her is to remove little by little everything that can take that heart away from Him, for she will never have the courage to break away herself. For, as far as you were concerned, that spiritual support replaced all others. God's jealousy would not tolerate this kind of sharing, even though it is not sinful. That is your heaviest cross, because the heart is threatened where it is most sensitive.

And we think we have the more right to be distressed about it, because of its apparent greater threat to our spiritual advancement. An error and an illusion of self-esteem! "Thy Will Be Done" in these kind of hardships gain for us more true virtue and more merit in the sight of

God than we could receive from the very best, worthy, saintly and consoling advice in the world. But if we followed this sound advice we would not commit so many faults. Those faults are less displeasing to God than the most trivial attachment to our own heart, however pure and innocent it may appear and truly is. And so I cannot sufficiently admire God's mercy to you, who has guided you for a number of years by these kind of deprivations in order to break down all spiritual dependence on yourself. Now He has also been attacking the body with infirmities, in order to detach you from yourself. He attacks the soul with worries, loathing, indifference and other trials, in order to detach it within from all support and all consolation in order that you should hold fast to Him alone with perfect faith and a pure heart. As St Francis de Sales says in the very depths of the spirit, "Leave all to God's mercy, you can safely trust Him." I must admit that the longer I live the more I see and understand that everything depends on God alone, and that we only have to leave everything to Him in order to succeed in everything. No sooner have I offered everything to Him than everything turns out as hoped for.

You are quite right to think that there are many with heavier crosses than yours. But you must realize that bearing this weight may not prevent our being deprived of a conscious and consoling submission, but never of a perfect faith and a pure heart, which no empty complacence can spoil. That is why God gives to many people only this last submissiveness, which leaves them suffering and humiliated beneath the burden of their affliction. God cuts the coat according to the cloth. We are always given special grace to overcome extraordinary difficulties. Everything we are unable to prevent becomes easier to endure through patience. It is what a pagan philosopher said by the sole light of reason, let alone any mention of faith or religion. Total submission to God can alone bring us great benefit and be our principal consolation.

LETTER 22

It is the devil who inspires so much anxiety and torment over discovering our suffering within, because he knows, by thousands of examples, that souls who have sufficient courage and humility to respond to these discoveries straightforwardly and honestly, are cured or at least greatly relieved.

Adhere to all the demands of Divine Providence in all circumstances both without and within; in sickness or in health, in indifference, aversion and temptation etc., absolutely and generally. That is truly to say from the heart: "Yes, my God, I desire everything, accept everything, I sacrifice everything to You, or at least I long to and I ask for Your grace. Help, strengthen and support my feebleness, and in the worst torments and temptations, my God, protect me from all sin. But as for the martyrdom within and the torments I feel, I accept it as much and for as long as it may please You. Thy will be done."

Concerning minor remedies, they must be willingly taken when necessary, according to the doctor's, superior's and nurse's orders. There is a greater self-denial in this through giving up one's own ideas, judgements and will.

This is another truth the ignorance of which causes many devout people to be unhumble in their humiliation, obstinately attached to their own ideas, and very opinionated in their saintly wishes. This is what ruins and corrupts all their saintly intentions. Oh, whoever discovered once and for all how to renounce their will, their judgement and their own ideas for the love of God, what progress would they not make in the path of sound and true perfection?

Nevertheless, only use your heart and your reason to discover what is demanded of you, act on it promptly, happily, in total confidence in God and abandonment to His mercy, knowing that you are fulfilling His Divine will. And so you must be obedient in everything no matter what the cost. That is everything, including mental and vocal prayers, offices, confessions, communions, etc. Blind obedience makes no exceptions. It is a willing sacrifice of our own spirit, our ideas, our judgement, inclination, repugnance, aversion, mood, in a word, of all our whims. So that this sacrifice is more pleasing to God than anything we could possibly do and that, without it, all the rest is of little use, often none at all, and nearly always harmful. Furthermore the Holy Spirit assures us in the scriptures that the obedient man will meet with victories.

The Cross of Communal Life

LETTER 23

You have reason, my dear Sister, to thank God for preserving peace, and charity and tenderness in your heart towards the person who is in charge of you. He is doing you a great favour in this. Perhaps He will further arrange that she, whether through ignorance, or inadvertance, or even, if you like, capriciously or through bad temper, will give you an opportunity of exercising patience. Ah, my Sister, try to make good use of these precious occasions, so propitious for winning God's heart.

Alas, we offend Him every day, this God of mercy, in so many ways; not only through ignorance or inadvertently, but deliberately and maliciously. We wish Him to pardon us, and in fact He does so very mercifully. But we do not wish to pardon those who are like us! Nevertheless, every day we say the prayer which Jesus Christ our Lord taught us, "Forgive us, Lord, as we forgive . . ." Let us remind ourselves again of God's great promise, that He will treat us as we treat our neighbour. So let us live as we treat our neighbours. So let us be tolerant, considerate, charitable, tender and sympathetic to our neighbour, and God, faithful to His promise, will do the same for you. I dwell on this subject because it will provide you each day with many occasions to practise the most exceptional and solid virtues of charity, patience, tenderness, humility, kindness, and the control of your temper, etc. These virtues, carried out faithfully, will bring you a rich harvest of grace and mercy for eternity. It is in this way more than by all other devices or means that you can attain the great benefit of prayer within, peace of heart, composure, and the continual presence of God and His perfect love. This single cross, borne patiently, will bring you countless mercies. It will be more helpful than seemingly heavier burdens, in completely detaching you from yourself in order that you may belong solely to God.

LETTER 24

I admit, my dear Sister, that there is nothing more difficult than to preserve perfect equanimity and inexhaustible patience in the face of domestic difficulties and clashes with people of different temperaments who surround us. These continual frustrations sometimes overwhelm us and make us unable to forget ourselves. But if we do fall for a moment, we recover. Succumbing is weakness – recovering is virtue. If we slip we pick ourselves up without any vexation, and little by little God gives everything to those who know how to wait on Him patiently.

But you want everything in a hurry, and you think you can become perfect all at once. You must try little by little to moderate and check that violent agitation whose turbulance threatens to break our heart. If we are unable to prevent this tumult let us at least try to suffer this misery unresistingly and patiently.

The trouble you are put to and the injustice shown to you are, I admit, sore trials. My heart revolts just to hear about it. But what other cure for that is there than the one which has already served us as a cure for many other ills – to raise our eyes to heaven saying, "Lord, it is Your will, You permit it. I adore and submit. Your holy will be done! Your divine permission allows me to carry Your cross which helps me to atone for my sins and deserve heaven." *Fiat, Fiat!*

If I knew a better cure I would tell you. But since I am sure that it is the most effective of all, you will allow me not to look for others. I grant that it is almost impossible on such occasions not to allow oneself to indulge in a little impatience and rebellion and bitterness, at least in our heart. But we must always return humbly to God and ourselves, without too much anguish, and immediately pray to him for the courage to do so.

LETTER 25

We must try to support one another with gentleness, humility and patience and try to profit from each other's errors, overcoming them as soon as we can. Otherwise we shall never have any peace.

I agree that your habitual circumstances are very hard, but also what a store of merit in heaven they provide! What a chance to repent and to act courageously and, in a short time, to reach that state of Grace of the life within if you only remain faithful to continual abnegation and self-denial in love, humility and abandonment to God. They are acts of virtue which will soon prepare your heart for the sweetest infusions of divine love, and I would be extremely sorry for you if you were in easier and more agreeable circumstances. This was really what the saints valued and sought, because they realized its great advantages for reforming within and for achieving true union with God.

You have been assailed for a long time by a temptation the more dangerous because you do not recognize it as such. The cause of it is that you have never really understood or examined the truth and the fundamental principle which is an article of faith: that everything that happens in this world, with the exception of sin alone, comes directly from God and by order of His will.

Therefore, though it is certain that God does not want sin, slanders, persecutions, injustices, etc., He does want their effect. That is to say, He wishes His elect to be slandered, persecuted, humiliated and even martyred in hundreds of ways. Furthermore, when a man by his own fault, through his imprudence and even by his sins, is striken with poverty, illness, and all manner of harsh afflictions, God – while He detests those faults, that imprudence, those sins – really wants the consequences. That is to say, He wants that poverty, sickness, loss of fortune and all other suffering, whatever it may be. That man then can and must say, "Lord, I have truly deserved it all. You allowed it, You wished it so that Your divine will might be fulfilled. I accept it all, I adore and submit." You have failed to understand the great precept that made that saintly man, Job, say, "God granted me favours, God took them from me. Blessed be His name." He did not say, "God granted me favours and Satan took them from me", for God alone allowed it. That was how Job was able to achieve perfect submission, courage, steadfastness and the peace of his soul. You have failed to grasp this fundamental truth. You have never been able to submit to certain situations and events, nor, consequently, to stand firm and at peace in the Will of God. Satan has always tempted, worried and upset you with hundreds of fantasies and false arguments on this subject. So try, I beg you, in the interests of your own salvation and peace, to overcome such spiritual aberrations which are the source of so much resentment, distress and heartfelt rebellion. For this you must get used to carrying out acts of faith and submission to all that originates from men or the devil's malice or from your own sins. God has allowed it, He is the Master, may He be blessed and His holy will accomplished! *Fiat! Fiat!*

Your situation is very painful, it is true, but for that very reason it is all the more sanctifying. It is the best possible penance you can do, being assured that it is God's will. Everything that the Devil puts into your heart to the contrary is obvious fantasy in order to deprive you of God's holy peace in you and you in God, in order to make you unhappy, upset and distressed, and always discontented with your present circumstances and always longing for a change. That is how he makes so many people in the world both unhappy and guilty by failing to submit to, or wish to understand, this is so important and consoling truth: that everything except sin is God's will, who arranges everything for His glory and for the greatest good of His creature if she realizes it and wishes to benefit from it in blind submission, total and general, without any exception or contradiction. O God, if I could only engrave this truth in your heart and in your spirit, engrave it, I repeat, with my blood. But God will do it Himself I feel sure! – little by little, if you will only co-operate with His mercy by promptly rejecting every thought to the contrary. One more thing, I beg of you. Rise above your own wishes, and obey the secret commands of that adorable Providence, and you will be sanctified in God's eyes.

LETTER 26

My dear Sister,
1. Do not burden yourself with vocal prayers other than
   obligatory ones, and apply yourself rather to perfecting
your inner life and to silent prayer.

2. It is very useful to forestall your faults with some acts of penitence. But it is preferable to atone for them after having committed them, than greatly to increase your acts of penitence beforehand when it may not be necessary.

3. Moderate and spiritualize your tenderness for those who are dear to you.

4. In order to strengthen your faith, profit from the good example and conversation of holy people without showing contempt or consciously indulging in distaste for others.

5. Do not blame yourself too much for being so often at grips with miserable nature. Heaven is worth all these battles. Perhaps they will be over quickly, and will soon bring you complete victory. In the end they will pass, and eternal peace will follow. Remain calm then, so that your humility may always be mixed with trust.

6. You must take advantage of bodily infirmities in order to strengthen your soul by surrendering to God's will and by union with Jesus Christ.

7. Remember to die to self, to renounce the flesh. On every occasion check your impatience and stifle your human feelings. This kind of mortification is most necessary. It is not harmful to health and is more effective than corporal mortification for increasing your merit and realizing the plans of God, who wants you to be all His own without exception or reservation.

8. Try faithfully but patiently to take advantage of all the different circumstances in which it pleases God to put you for His glory and your perfection. Turn in perfect love and total obedience to the fatherly guidance of Divine Providence.

9. It is necessary that eagerness for our own improvement and that of those in our charge, be ardent and active, but never hurried or accompanied by trouble and doubt.

10. Try to become more and more spiritual, steadfastly aspiring to all the perfection of your saintly vocation. Humble yourself ceaselessly before God in order to gain victory over yourself. You need very powerful help so that your sensitivity, your human and only too natural diffidence, are completely extinguished before you die. These faults derive from your character and your temperament. It is true that these considerations partly excuse them and arouse the compassion of our dear Lord for His poor spouse; but, nevertheless, fight on so that if your wretched pride and human vanity have not been totally extinguished before your last hour, at least death will find you trying to destroy them. Your principal weapons must be divine love and infinite gratitude for God's mercy, a simple trust in Him and a profound mistrust of yourself, always without despair and at peace. You will derive an ever growing strength from Holy Communion, prayer, humility, tenderness, patience, obedience, mortification and above all self-denial within.

11. Sickness and infirmity, in total submission to God's will, and a humble act of grace and union with Jesus Christ, will greatly help to expiate the past and weaken the

old man. They will help you to die spiritually before dying naturally. Which, by ending our temporary suffering, will bring us hopefully to the enjoyment of eternal bliss. When God himself tests us with this kind of penitence, not being able to mortify ourselves outwardly we must compensate by mortification within: setting ourselves more and more to destroying self-love, pride, fastidiousness and criticism which are its rotten fruits. Finally, try to become humble and simple as a little child for the love of and in imitation of our Lord, in a peaceful and contemplative mood. If God sees that we are humble He will promote his work in us. Perseverance and faith in His mercy for the greater glory of God all depends on truly loving this God of mercy in your heart and in your actions.

12. As our journey progresses on this earthly pilgrimage let us earnestly try to grow in true ardour, in keeping with the perfection of our saintly calling and with God's special plans for us. When He gives us certain ideas and inclinations, let us profit from them over and above all His other gifts in order to come closer to Him. But at times of dryness, let us continue as usual on our way, humbly recalling helplessness, believing that perhaps God may be testing our love for Him by some beneficial trials.

13. Let us but be truly and humbly concerned to correct our own faults and we will rarely give a thought to those of others. Let us see Jesus Christ in all our neighbours and we shall have no difficulty in forgiving them, to stand by them and cherish them. His example invites us: what patience with His ignorant and coarse disciples! Let us devote all our ardour to glorifying God who lives in us and in those whom He sends to influence us. Let us live hidden

in Jesus Christ, and die to all creation and to ourselves. Otherwise Jesus Christ would not consent to live in us, or not at any rate in the way He claims to, by absorbing all our human life in His divine life. For the rest let us sustain ourselves by love as we do others, always humbling ourselves and immediately punishing ourselves for our sins. When we pray for ourselves let us also pray for others.

Work and Employment

LETTER 27

I have already told you many times, my dear Sister, that nothing should trouble us, not even our misdeeds. All the more reason why we must never allow ourselves to be defeated by the distressing consequences of certain things we have done and which are not sins, even though they may imply some imprudence on our part. Few trials are as mortifying to our pride and, consequently, there are few more sanctifying than these. It costs us very little more to accept these humiliations which come from without and for which we are not in the least responsible. We can resign ourselves much more easily to the shame caused by faults graver in themselves, provided they are not apparent. But a slight imprudence resulting in tiresome consequences, obvious to everyone, is certainly the most humiliating of all humiliations; and therefore an excellent occasion for destroying pride. Never fail to take advantage of it. Taking our heart in both our hands, we force it, in spite of its resistance, to make an act of penance. It is then that we must say obediently again and again, "Thy Will be done", and even force ourselves to add an act of grace and say

"Glory be to God!" As to what follows in respect to God, having been of yourself its cause, although innocent, remain undeterred in your determination to take at a suitable time the necessary steps for peace and union of hearts, leaving the outcome to God whatever it may be.

Let us accustom ourselves to do the same in all distressing occasions of our miserable existence. We shall then deserve to rest in peace on the bosom of Divine Providence. Without this total submission there is no hope of peace during this sad pilgrimage. Let us think only of pleasing God, sacrificing everything to Him. Let all else go to hell; provided God remains in us there is nothing to lose.

I am neither vexed nor worried about inward suffering. Only have courage and all will be well. Do not worry or be surprised at this rebellion in your heart. I assure you that this in no way hinders your spiritual surrender. God has His reasons for concealing it.

During the most violent feelings of revolt try only to say these few words: "It is quite right that the creature be obedient to her God! Anyway I wish it and desire it!"

Read page nine of Father Guillore's *Progress in the Life Within*. This chapter is divine. I hope you will be completely drenched in it and take it to heart. In the name of God, do not fret yourself. Try to maintain a foundation of peace in the midst of the most terrible storms, and all will be well. In fact, I can see nothing but good in all you have disclosed to me; but a good that will cease to be if it were known to you as God has made it known to me.

When hundreds of different thoughts assail me, magnifying the most trivial things until they become monsters, I remember what I tell others in a similar situation. I adandon myself to Providence in and for everything, and to Jesus Christ, without whose mercy we can do nothing and without union with whom our sacrifices are nothing in the eyes of God. And so I beseech Him to protect me from all temptations and all sin. I accept for all time, as long as He wills it, bitterness of heart, inner torment, spiritual degradation, contempt of others with all that follows. And I beseech Him to preserve me from saying or doing anything to elude the least of His wishes. I accept it for as long as it pleases Almighty God, wishing that His holy will be accomplished even to the prejudice of mine. I beseech Him to prevent me from saying or doing anything to elude the least of His wishes. And even if, through weakness, in error, or though malice, I were to do so, I beseech Him to prevent me from succeeding. I admit that all His wishes are not only holy and adorable but infinitely beneficial to His humble and obedient creatures, and that mine, on the contrary, are always blind and unruly. Thus, I fully subscribe to all that is recorded and written in the decrees of our heavenly Father. It is that Father, so dear and so holy, who has ordained it. That is enough. So what have I to fear? From this, two things emerge.

1. That during these tempests and storms, arising often out of nothing, I must maintain such a profound peace that I surprise even myself.

2. That I must consider myself fortunate to have suffered these temptations and trials. Then I say to myself, "This is worth more than all my own petty interests. I feel that my soul is so strengthened by submission to Divine Providence that all desire and all attachment to my own will is sacrificed and annihilated."

LETTER 28

It is the greatest blessing to witness the bad behaviour of others without contempt, indignation or impatience, and even without worrying. If for some good reason you mention it, watch over your heart and your tongue, so that nothing escapes that God does not approve of. Say nothing except from good motives. Inwardly groan and humbly regret faults which can often slip into such exchanges. From time to time ask God for caution and charity, and then remain untroubled.

Cherish the saintly wish to belong wholly to God. Pray with faith, confidence and submission; above all deeply humbling yourself before God. It is for Him to complete the work He has begun in you. Nothing else will succeed. Many sacrifices must be made before God fills our hearts with the infinite joy of His perfect love. Since our hearts could not exist without love and affection let us pray and long for it. Only God's love enchants, upholds, possesses and converts them. Let us abandon ourselves unreservedly to God. Let us leave all to His benevolent Providence. Think only of walking resolutely in the path of the present, eternally decreed to be the surest way to our pre-destination. The actual continual fulfilment of God's will is the best time spent during our life.

LETTER 29

The wish for the perfection of our fellow creatures is no doubt excellent. The pain within caused by their failings is also very good and comes from the wish to see them perfect. But, under this pious pretext the devil or your own spirit have given you very damaging illusions, to others as well as to you. I can see no other remedy for you than the one which it has pleased God to inspire in me, for someone else suffering from more or less similar agitations and illusions and indiscreet and uncontrollable zeal. And so I order you, in the sacred name of Jesus Christ and His divine mother, no longer to think of pursuing misguided remedies. I adjure you before God. This is what you must tell Him, especially when the devil is trying to arouse your zeal. "Lord," you will say, "Charity is the queen of virtues. I must therefore no longer pursue that of zeal except when you help me to do so without corrupting the love I owe to others and myself. When I find myself strong enough, or rather humble enough, to be zealous with profound peace in my soul, with gentleness, compassion and understanding towards my neighbour; with sympathy, love and charity which nothing can turn sour or scandalize except our own faults; with a patience and forbearance which enables us quietly to endure the faults of others and for as long as you do, O God — may we not be worried or troubled or astonished at their incorrigibility.

When God has put you in this saintly and right frame of mind, you will be able to, and should, resume your enthusiasm. Until then, think only of yourself and know that God, in order to punish others and to cure them of imprudent, angry and sour zeal, has often allowed them to commit greater faults than those which they find scandalous in others.

Secondly, I command you never to speak of God, or of anything sacred, except in the spirit of tenderness, in a tolerant and gracious manner, with moderation and approval. But being in no way critical or severe. For, although you only repeat what is in the Gospel and the finest books, I can see that in your present frame of mind you exaggerate everything, either in its meaning, carrying things to the extreme, or in the turn of phrase. Nourish yourself and others with the infinite bounty of God, the trust we must have in Him, with the enthusiasm of a virtue which in no way embarrasses ourselves or others. Above all be very careful never to judge others harshly. If you have nothing gentle to say remain silent and leave others to make unprejudiced decisions, but none that can be called or appear to be harsh, which only offend the spirit and sour the heart instead of winning it over. Otherwise we do more harm than good, and disillusion rather than edify.

All this will help you a great deal in carrying out your duties in the Novitiate, and in practising the queen of virtues, Charity, so essential and especially recommended for anyone living in a community. It assures them that Charity operates always without risk, but that zeal is a very fragile virtue, full of pitfalls requiring care, reservation and caution, of which few people are capable. Above all, before correcting others we must have enough care and zeal to correct ourselves. Let him who is without sin, says Jesus Christ, cast the first stone.

LETTER 30

The peace of Jesus Christ be with you! You are right to try to maintain yourself in a state of perfect resignation and total obedience to God's wishes. It is in that which consists all perfection. But on this point, as in all others, you must distinguish between two kinds of resignation. One is appealing, inwardly attractive, peaceful and pleasing. The other is dry, tasteless and inwardly repelling, like the one you have told me of. The first is good, very agreeable to our nature, and so even a little dangerous, since it is quite natural to attach oneself to what is to one's taste. The second is painful, but however disagreeable it may be to our pride, is more perfect and deserving and in no way dangerous, because we can only delight in it through perfect faith and pure love. Try then, to act on these assumptions. Because when we accustom ourselves to act only according to our own performance and convictions, if these fail us we give up and become indifferent. But if we act in faith it never fails us. It is in order gradually to make us act in accordance with these last motives that God often deprives us of feelings and inclinations without which we would never grow up. And so you must not be surprised by these worries, dislikes, rebellions, etc, which you tell me about. God allows them for your own good. Should you dread that He will interfere with the human motives for the violence you are doing to yourself, tell yourself two things: "I am now in no condition to judge. We will think it over calmly when we are at peace. As long as there remains something human in me God allows it, in order to help my frailty. When it has pleased Him to make me less imperfect, we will behave more perfectly." Thereupon, calm yourself and do not allow yourself to worry willingly.

I can easily understand the distaste your vocation inspires in you. But think of the Martyrs' crowns! It is natural, then, to feel doubly drawn to the solitary life; but a life of obedience is worth even more. It is a continual sacrifice. Cling ever closer to it so that you will not do anything which might detach you from the Cross of Jesus Christ.

The great secret of how to endure these miseries patiently and serenely is this:

1. To look upon one's misery as God's cross, just like illness and other misfortunes of life. And since we endure these patiently let us endure those others in the same way.

2. To look upon suffering as the rewards of a spiritual life, because it is the chief way of acquiring humility and a distrust of oneself.

In this light, delight in humiliation and self-abasement as St Francis de Sales says. But should it not be hidden so as not to edify? – All the better! Simply try quite calmly to behave so that those unworthy sentiments are not apparent externally. Yet should they be apparent through no fault of your own, try to appear undismayed by this seeming humiliation and baseness. And even if they are your own fault, detesting the cause – as says your blessed Father – adore, for the love of God, the humiliation that comes with it. For if we are not careful, we only wish to avoid outward faults in order to avoid a little humiliation.

To calm your worry over not knowing what to think about, remember that often the wish for habitual meditation alone can do so, and that you have only to long unceasingly to think of God, to please God, to obey God, in order, in effect, to think of pleasing and obeying Him.

You say that the more you pray the less you know how to. This may very well be because your longing in some way lacks humility and purity of intention. Always say your prayers with the single desire to please God and to be consoled. Say them in a spirit of sacrifice in order to experience everything that is pleasing to Him. Know that contemplative prayers are of a kind that escapes us if we strive to hold on to them, but remain with us if we are able to maintain a certain indifference to them. It is the doctrine according to St Francis de Sales.

You should frequently recall this great principle: that great misery and spiritual suffering, fully recognized, deeply felt, and truly welcomed because we cherish our helplessness, is one of the greatest treasures, because it maintains us in profound humility. But to think we are lost because we have none of these sentiments and imagine ourselves to be without faith, hope or charity, etc.; and therefore to worry, despair and lose heart, is an illusion, a temptation, our pride that always wants to understand everything. We must then say to ourselves: "I have been, I am, I shall always be whatever is pleasing to God. But, in my reason and in the depths of my heart, I wish to and will be His, cost or happen to me what may, in this world or the next."

You will not be able to explain to me what you are feeling. But I will tell you. On the one hand it is all manner of revolts, temptations, and a perpetual confusion within aroused by the devil and your pride. On the other, it is a little ray of light in what is called the upper part of the spirit, and faith, scarcely perceptible on account of the turbulence in the lower part. And with that frail support you are unshakeable because the thread in God's hand is as strong as a cable, and a single hair stronger than an iron chain.

It is a temptation and misguided humility to withdraw from the sacraments. What others do should be of no consequence to you. You do not know either their feelings, or their motives, or the cause of their withdrawal.

You say that God often deprives you of the feeling of

grace. To which of His beloved friends has He ever given continually this tangible support? Do you, by chance, presume to be more privileged than many saints, from whom He has removed it more often and for longer than from you? What was left to them then other than the single light of faith, and a faith like our own which seems to us to be darkness? And in their temptations and troubled passions they knew no more than we do, whether God was pleased with them. Faith alone teaches us, apart from special revelations, and the saints themselves could never be sure; and you complain that you cannot be either! That is where your wretched pride has brought you. In order to satisfy it God would have to work miracles! Of all the misery that so humiliates you that is certainly the greatest and the most fitted to humble you.

To wish to be disinterested in ourselves so as to be interested in God alone, and continually to fall back on oneself, is, I admit, a temptation as harassing as flies in autumn. These temptations must be continually brushed away, just as we continually brush away the flies without ever tiring from this labour, quietly, however, without any stress or strain.

We must humble ourselves before God as we do in other difficulties.

It is ourselves who force God to overwhelm us with misery in order to make us humble and to despise ourselves. If, in spite of this, we have so little humility and so much pride, how would we feel if we found ourselves exempt from these miseries?

Believe me, for a long time it has seemed to me that you have been so overcome with misery that I regard this alone to be one of the most merciful acts of grace God could have conferred upon you. Cherish, therefore, everything that will preserve it. I am wholly yours in our Saviour. Actually I am tired of writing so much. Before reading the end of your letter I had the same idea as you, of dividing up my replies to your questions. However, now I don't regret having enabled you to grasp at one glance what you must do in order to benefit from the trials to which God has subjected you.

The Cross Within

LETTER 31

1. I understand from what you tell me that you are walking in darkness. To begin with, you must realize that this is fairly common in people of your sex, and that it is the safest way because it is less open to vain complacence and pride and vanity. So this darkness itself is a gift of God, because the best way of walking with God is by faith alone, which is always obscure.

2. In spite of this darkness we can understand and describe it clearly enough to any experienced director. You tell me you are unable to pray. Experience has taught me that people with good intentions who speak in this way know how to pray better than others, because their prayers are more simple and more humble. Owing to their simplicity they are more spontaneous. To pray in this manner is to remain firm in faith in the presence of God, with a secret and continual longing to receive God's grace according to our needs. Because as God knows all our wishes, this, says St Augustine, is our main prayer. Wishing always is praying always. If your prayer is simple, it cannot

ask too much. God loves to see us as poor little children at His feet.

3. The strength we receive from Holy Communion and holy hunger for that divine food are a strong reason for taking them often. There is no need for you to worry about this, I assure you.

4. Indifference to things of this world and even detachment from parents is a greater mercy than you imagine. There is nothing else left but to be detached from ourselves by a total self-denial, above all within. Frequent union with Jesus Christ and prayer will achieve this little by little, provided you wish for it yourself by ceaselessly forgetting yourself in order to think of God, abandoning to Him all your spiritual and worldly interests.

5. You are told, quite rightly, that God only demands your total obedience and resignation to everything. Ah, my dear sister, therein lies the whole of perfection! It is error and illusion to search for anything else. And so, someone who is spiritual and somewhat withdrawn need, truth tell, only do one thing, and that is to make a simple submission and adherence of heart to every imaginable situation, be it within or without, in which God wishes to put her. For instance, you are ill; God wishes it. Say, then, "Very Well! I wish it too, in the same way and as long as He does." – "But perhaps that will make me incapable of work or serving the community?" Well again! "If God wishes it I do too, and I accept in advance, together with the Cross of Suffering I am enduring, the holy shame and humiliation that goes with it." "But perhaps in this situation I am a little lenient with myself and do not do

76

myself the violence I ought to and could?" "But even in this, after consulting my superior and my confessor, I allow their judgement. It is the will of God and so I wish it too." And so let us remain tranquil in all these divine wishes and in the peace within where God operates. Therein lies, my sister, your great and only way. Follow it faithfully and continually. Reject all contrary thoughts and ideas, as though they were suggested by the devil, who wishes at any rate to destroy the peace within you, which is the good of your soul and the firm foundation of spiritual life.

6. You have been very imprudent and disobedient in exposing yourself to the risk of three months of fever. God's just punishment! Acknowledge that this refusal to make the best of your circumstances, is not in any way virtuous, but mere stubbornness and obstinate attachment to one's opinion and wilfulness, under a pious pretext. Most of our religious and spiritual sisters arouse our pity in similar circumstances and one needs to be very patient with them. It is blindness and illusion, from which perhaps even an angel from heaven would find difficulty in saving them. As for you, submit to everything, listen to everything, suffer everything in peace with meekness and patience, and remain like that in all that God wills. That is the greatest blessing for you.

7. It is quite right that you should not be allowed to leave your employment or to think of doing so. I also shall do everything in my power to prevent you. Be careful not to go against God's command. "But I am not strong enough." God will give you the strength if it is necessary. "But I am not capable enough." God will never lack the power to give it you, and if He has given you the greater

part, which is mistrust of yourself in this respect, a recognition and an awareness of your capability, that is the essential. For then we rely only on God, we call on Him in everything, we attribute nothing to ourselves but everything to God alone, and His blessing alone makes all things increase and grow. Briefly, rest in peace and confidence on this God of love, and despair as much as you like. And so always remain humble about your own incapacity, weakness and foolishness. It is just such means as this that it pleases God to use in order visibly to demonstrate His glory.

8. There is no need to worry over your doubts about religious truths. They are not a bad mark in respect of certain souls. On the contrary, it is often a sign that God wishes to lead them in the surer path of pure and simple faith, without those sentiments and delights which He gives when He pleases. Waiting on God requires no effort or violence, except against sin, but rather peace and contentment. When you are unable to succeed in making an act of faith, say to yourself: "Ah well! Everything is done in the eyes of God. Because He has seen my desire, He will enable me to do so when He pleases. He is the Master. May only His Holy Will always be my own, for I am only in this world to accomplish it. It is my wealth and my treasure. Let God give the others enlightenment, mercies, gifts, sweet spiritual awareness, as much as it may please Him. For myself I only wish to be rich if that is His wish." There, my dear sister, is your way. If you walk in it peacefully, confidently, and in total self-denial, you will walk safely.

9. The greatest concern for your progress must consist above all in suffering, without protest, everything that God wishes or allows to happen to you, without complaining and begging for sympathy from others. Don't waste time in idle talk or even entertain futile plans for the future which may never be as you imagine it. Beware of all that empties you of God. Be on your guard against it.

10. In order to make it easier to keep your thoughts continually on God in accordance with your wish and your need, this is what you must do. First, love solitude and silence, which greatly help the spirit within, and sacred meditation. Second, choose only to read books that are sound and full of piety. Pause frequently, trying to appreciate rather than understand or remember them. Third, throughout the day make fervent prayers to God about all that takes place: during temptation, affliction, worry, disgust, sourness of heart, disagreements and so on.

11. Your prayers to God for indifference to everything are inspired by His grace. Continue and rest assured that sooner or later they will be answered.

LETTER 32

1. All will be well in time. Let us remain at peace before God and always submit to His holy will, whose accomplishments must determine and limit all our wishes.

2. I am a little surprised that, in spite of my direction, you have so long been unaware of what takes place in God's creatures. God, you say, does not inspire what causes our

downfall. This is true in one sense. But isn't it also true that God has often allowed misunderstandings, and still does, in order to test, influence, crucify and sanctify one person through another? We see hundreds of examples of this in the lives of St Regis and of the venerable Sister Marguerite-Marie Alacoque. Let us try to judge everything, not with our feeble, limited and blind human judgement, but according to the judgement of Divine Providence which is so enlightened, right, sure and infallible. In this way everything could edify us without ever troubling our peace of mind and heart. It is by continual sacrifices and a total abandon to Divine Providence that we work surely for our eternal salvation and our progress in virtue, more than by anything else. It is in this that strong and genuine love of God consists, without which all the rest is merely frivolous and often an empty dream.

LETTER 33

Believe me, dear sister, we must suppress all our fears and rely for everything on Divine Providence, who has secret but infallible means of achieving all His own ends. Whatever men say or do, they do nothing but what God wishes or allows, or which He does not use for the accomplishment of His own merciful designs. He is no less able to achieve His ends in the most apparently unlikely ways, than He is to refresh His servants in the middle of a blazing furnace by making them walk on water. We are all the more aware of this fatherly protection of Providence when we commit ourselves to it with childlike trust.

I have just, only quite recently, experienced this. I also prayed God, more fervently than ever, to do me the grace never to grant my wishes, which are always blind and often pernicious; but always His, which are just, holy, loving and infinitely beneficial. Ah, if you knew how delightful it is only to find happiness and rest in the sole accomplishment of the will of God, as holy as He is powerful, you could never wish for anything else! Never look upon suffering, whatever it may be, as a sign of estrangement from God; because crosses and torments, whether without or within, are all, on the contrary, the result of His bounty and a sign of His love.

But, you ask, what will become of me if . . . ? Oh, those are truly temptations of the enemy! Why are we so simple as to torment ourselves in advance about what perhaps may never happen? Sufficient for the day is its evil! Pessimistic predictions are very harmful; why surrender to them so easily? We are indeed enemies of our peace, since, what do we gain by that and, on the other hand, what we do not lose for time and eternity? When we are possessed, in spite of ourselves, with harassing forebodings, we must faithfully make continual sacrifices to our sovereign Lord. This is what I beg you to do. In this way you will be engaging God in your favour to help you in everything. You will gain a store of wealth and credit in heaven, a submission and an abandon which will bring you closer to God than any other pious practices, and it looks as though it is with this in view that God allows you to have all this imaginary suffering and torment. Profit by them and God will bless you. Your acceptance of any hardships, whatever it pleases Him to inflict on you, alone will help you more than the finest talk and the most holy book. If you could understand this great truth, what peace within and what progress on the road to God! Without this falling in with His wishes, all spirituality counts for little. As long as we limit ourselves to outward acts of piety, we can only have a thin crust of true and solid piety within, which consists essentially in wishing for everything, everywhere, what God wishes and how He wishes it. When we achieve this, God's Spirit alone reigns in our heart, and never fails to supply our needs when we call on Him in humble trust.

This is a fact of faith, but alas, it is too little known to a great many otherwise pious souls. And they are often to be seen crawling or halting on their way to God. What pitiful blindness! The difficulties and troubles we find ourselves in, by God's order and the arrangements of wise and divine Providence, are equal to the sweetest meditation if we are able often to repeat, from the bottom of our heart, "Lord, You wish it, I wish it, *fiat*!" What if we do only say it from the bottom of our heart, as St Francis de Sales says, and our will appears to play no part? – the sacrifice is only more acceptable to God and more spiritually rewarding to us.

Cling steadfastly to this practice and you will taste its delicious fruits. If you can add a measure of peace and tranquillity, a certain gentleness of heart towards others and yourself, without ever showing any sign of contempt, impatience or ill temper, what great and worthy sacrifices will you not make. At least, gently humble yourself after each of your faults, and turn to God in confidence as though all was well, as the "spiritual battle" teaches us. Since we can enjoy neither happiness nor peace in this miserable life, except in so far as we blindly obey the orders of Divine Providence, I never tire of telling you about it. Believe me, rely on that loving Divine Providence and abandon all care for anything else. Do only with simplicity what you think you should in all situations so as not to tempt God. But do it gently, quietly, effortlessly, without trouble, without hurry or worry, as says St Francis de

Sales. Good Lord! How much uneasiness, regret and foreboding do we not gradually avoid, by this very reasonable and Christian conduct!

1. Your ordeal of suffering is very painful, but very favourable for heaven. The ideas of men differ and they vary according to their own interests, each one full of his own ideas, imagining that all reason is on his side. O men, O men! What have we come to? What have we come to? What depths of humiliation for all mankind! Let us accustom ourselves to recognize the depths of truth in everything. The spirit, lit by faith, disposes the heart to submit to the arrangements of Divine Providence, which allow good people to endure suffering in order to separate them from others. In these circumstances we have only religion and submission to God that can uphold us, as much for our own sakes as for the sake of those who influence us, about whom we so easily worry under the misguided pretext of reason. But know that there is never any reason for us to allow ourselves to be disheartened, worried or disturbed by anything whatever. These unruly impulses are always contrary to reason and to faith.

2. For the rest, it is allowed to talk in confidence to a director in order to control and reassure ourselves and to learn; but always with discretion and charity. Nevertheless, more important would be silence and to talk only to God and tell Him, as you would a friend or a most trustworthy director. This is an excellent and easy prayer. It is called a prayer of trust and outpouring of the heart

before God. We are fortified within and draw from it great consolation, peace of heart and courage.

As long as you live more or less as you do, although very imperfectly, but with a sincere wish and trying hard to do better, you are assured of salvation. Even doubt itself is a gift of God, as long as it doesn't go so far as distressing you and making you reluctant to take the sacraments or to practise virtue and your spiritual excercises. As for the hardness and indifference of heart about which you complain, be patient and offer this suffering to God in a spirit of penitence, as you offer Him illnesses and bodily weakness. Those of the soul are harder to bear and as a result more beneficial.

LETTER 35

I would agree it is true that one would have to be a saint to put away such things, and that it would be better never to take them up. But, in such exceptional circumstances, try first of all to remove as far as you can all thoughts, feelings and talk which could sour your heart. When you cannot get rid of them (or can do so only partially) say in your heart or deep in your soul, "But God, You have allowed it: Your holy and adorable wishes, Your divine permission are accomplished in all that happens! I offer You this sacrifice of suffering and all its consequences. They will all be to Your liking; You are the Master. Thanks be to you for and in everything. *Fiat!*" Add as well: "I pardon, Lord, with all my heart for love of You, the person who has been the cause of my suffering, and as a sign of my sincerity about my feelings for her, ask You for all kinds of mercy, blessing and happiness for her." If your heart offers any resistance, say, "Lord, You see my misery, but at least I wish for it and I beg You to grant me that mercy." This done, think no more about it, or suffer as God may please without withdrawing your sacrifice. This is one of the great ways of sharing the chalice of Jesus Christ, our Master.

LETTER 36

Notice how Divine Providence takes a hand in our affairs, down to the smallest detail, and is able to provide admirably for everything. When it is contrary to our wishes our blind pride makes us defiant and we even start complaining. But then God acts like a good father who loves His children, and gives them the bitter medicines which are necessary to purge them. Leave it to Him, and we, the poor blind, let us never argue with His wise Providence or against His arrangements, which are always infinitely loving and beneficial to whoever accepts them from the paternal hand with true submission and childlike awe. All that you tell me about the various impressions, often contradictory, and about the alternating inclinations you experience during the Mission is what everyone experiences in similar circumstances, each after their own fashion. It is what are called vicissitudes which we must expect, just as we do changes in the seasons, the weather, the days and their different hours. In all that, you need only one single act of submission, one single *Fiat*.

I have often told you, and I repeat it again: God wishes to make you penitent, and above all to save you by heartbreak and inward suffering, and more especially by pangs of conscience, and by the various inward doubts which He so often makes you experience. All I ask of you in these trials is a little submission and abandonment, more or less such as you have in other misfortunes of life, in disasters, illness, infirmities, and so forth. As far as your confessions are concerned, rest – assured blind obedience can never mislead you.

As regards repentance, which is most essential, while adding to all your confessions some sin from your past life, be content to know that the surest sign of true repentance is not to fall into grievous sins and always to strive to correct and diminish lighter ones. And so remain untroubled, frail as you are, patiently enduring the various torments which take the place of fasts, discipline, hair shirt and cropped head, only with this difference: that in these penances your own will can play a part, whereas in the others, it is purely God's will and the penances which the heavenly Father gives those for whom He especially wishes salvation.

LETTER 37

1. As regards your confession: if the preparation takes more than half an hour, and making them longer than a quarter of an hour, that is too long. Do not worry about your repentance. By the mercy of God you have not fallen into anything approaching mortal sin. As for the past, by God's grace you have reformed. The surest sign the Church can give.

2. Try to remember frequently this great proposition: God has put, and could only have put, me in this world to acknowledge, love and serve Him. I wish always to do

Him the least possible harm. Moreover, He will make of me what He pleases, and I submit totally to His holy will, who only wishes for my salvation, and making me eternally happy in the life to come. It is for this alone that He has the goodness to make me endure much suffering inwardly and outwardly. May He be for ever blessed!

3. You must see your past, present and perhaps future sufferings with respect to your confessions as a penance from the heavenly Father, since I am certain that in your general confession you say and intend to say everything. That is sufficient. All the more so since, I judge before God, that in the whole of this confession no serious omission can be found. And so remain in peace and undisturbed about it.

4. As for those sublime dispositions you so admire but which you dare not even wish for, here are two remedies (a) Humble yourself and groan inwardly but remain calm and unworried at seeing yourself so far removed from those saintly dispositions. (b) Hope inwardly to be able to desire them, since little by little one passes from one degree to another, and from the faintest or half-wish, to a real wish, which by virtue of being renewed and remaining in the heart, strengthens itself and finally takes root there.

LETTER 38

1. True contrition which remits sin is entirely spiritual. It is true that on certain and many special occasions it can sometimes be conscious and very flattering to pride. But

this in no way depends on ourselves and is not at all essential or necessary. More often contrition is spiritual and the anxieties that arise from it are the best penance that can be offered to God because that is how He wishes it.

2. The power of this suffering is often not realized. We must trust in God and abandon ourselves to Him, after having done what we should, and when a wise and attentive confessor is satisfied with what we have done.

3. Being sometimes impressed and moved, and then to find ourselves at intervals callous does not depend on ourselves. These are inward vicissitudes. *Fiat, Fiat!* Therein lies the whole remedy. It is certain and a matter of faith that God always gives us support. Not the most perceptible, the most agreeable or the most desirable, but the most essential, which are often the least comprehensible and the most mortifying, in order to help us do better to ourselves.

4. God arranges and disposes of everything as it pleases Him, and uses whomever He needs for the success of His designs, as and when He chooses. So let us learn to abandon ourselves to Him in and for everything, submissively and confidently, as to one who can do all things and who disposes of everything according to His plans and His wishes. And in his frame of mind let us see that we follow the footsteps of Divine Providence rather than the path of our own activities and interests. Abandonment to this heavenly Providence pledges God to redeem all things, provide all things and console us in all things. Let us always remind ourselves of this proposition: everything passes but God remains!

Abandon yourselves, then, and all those who are precious and most dear to you, to the care of His loving Providence in public calamities as in all others, and we shall be able one day to say with David: "We rejoice, O Lord, for the years of affliction through which You have made us pass and, by means of a little short-lived suffering, You have saved our souls. Suffering is the lot of the chosen." Again let us say with the same prophet: "Lord, I have been silent and humble because it is You who made me." There are no other means of consolation in the greatest suffering than faith, religion, eternity, the sight of our sins being expiated in the short duration of our suffering, the immensity of rewards for those who patiently endured them. Impatience alone could redouble our suffering, just as patience alone can soften it. In every country in the world, God has His special scourges, which are like different rods with which He threatens and punishes our disobedience. But like a father, He scolds and beats us in this world, the better to save us for the next. May He be for ever blessed!

LETTER 39

Could you not cease your fears and alarms after all the experience of your errors, these unnecessary anxieties, especially those that deeply affect your heart. Try at least always to profit by your inward sacrifices and by your acceptance of all the orders of Divine Providence, whatever they may be. Await the success of all your own efforts and industry. But most of all those of God, counting only on His paternal love.

I agree with you, and I have never wished or asked for

punishment or conflicts. Those which Providence sends are enough without our wanting to procure them ourselves. We must await and prepare for them. It is a means by which we can have more strength and more courage to receive and sustain them as we should when God sends them. One of my most cherished habits, which I find profitable for this world and the next, is rejecting in advance, without question, everything that comes into my mind, but profiting by it when God crucifies us with these ideas and anxieties about the future. I have also always thought, when He sends us some few consolations, whether spiritual or temporal, that we should gratefully accept them, without depending on them or becoming too attached to them or enjoying them too much. All joy which is not in God is in vain and only nourishes our pride.

Your loneliness during the absence of [Her Director], tiresome though it may be, appears to me to be excellent for you. What acts of resignation in your frailty and helplessness! What raising up of the heart to God! What good feelings and noble resolutions! Good will will save you; God sees it in your heart. Each one has his way which he must follow according to his lights. Try, little by little, to make use of your present situation and your bitterness of heart, and to place all your confidence for the affairs of this world and eternity in God alone!

The sad picture which you paint of the present calamities makes it necessary, for your own peace of mind, to make to God unceasing sacrifices of public catastrophes, and for you to share in them. But the life of sinful men, as we all are, must be lived entirely in penitence and the cross, and God in His mercy offers us the cure which we must accept. The cup is bitter, it is true, but the flames of hell and purgatory are infinitely more so. Since we must drink this cup whether we like it or not, we make, as the proverb has it, necessity a virtue and virtue a necessity. This in itself will sweeten all our bitterness. The sufferings within are, as you say, the most agonizing, but they are also the most beneficial and purifying. And after this purification and detachment within, all is sweetened and made easier by submission and confidence in God alone through Jesus Christ our Lord.

Your thoughts about this are truly reasonable and just. But they are too human. We must always come back to abandonment and hope in Divine Providence alone. For what can men do, and what turn of the tide are they not exposed to? Let us count on God alone, then, who never changes, who knows better than we do what we need, and who gives it to us like a good father – but to children who are often so blind that they do not know what they are asking, even in their prayers, which seem to them most just and reasonable but which are short-sighted. They are wrong to look for all that happens in the future, its circumstances and its outcome, for that belongs to God alone. When He takes from us something that to us seems to be necessary, He knows how and is able to replace it in hundreds of different ways, unknown to us. This is so true that the bitterness and the heartbreak bravely endured, patiently and silently, inwardly and outwardly, benefit the soul more than do the instructions of the most saintly and clever director. I have had hundreds of examples. This is what you must do now and the only thing God demands of you: give obedience, abandon, trust, sacrifice and silence, in the best way you can, but without, however, making too violent efforts.

LETTER 40

To soften your suffering and sorrow, my dear sister, I have only two things to say to you. Everything comes from God. And on our part, everything consists of obeying the will of God. Whether we like it or not His will will always be accomplished. Let us unite ourselves to it with all the strength of our own will, and from then on we have nothing to fear. The heart pangs and uncontrolled rebellion only serve to add to the value of your submission. When we doubt whether we have any, we ask God to give it to us by saying inwardly: Lord, I wish and long for that total submission, and I offer you the heart-break that is tormenting me, as did the blood-stained agony of Jesus Christ, Your dear Son.

You must try slowly to discard all those useless reflections which only sour the heart. When, in spite of yourself, you are bitter, you must bear the pain patiently. When we are impatient it is then that we must make great efforts to be patient with our impatience itself, and to resign ourselves to the lack of submissiveness. Read, in the books *The Saints' Way to the Cross*, the chapters which describe your present state of mind. In them you will discover all the directions, supports and consolations you can possibly find. But don't expect to find what no man on earth knows how to give you. God alone can relieve you of your trials. Await His hour patiently. You have always depended too much on human help. God deprives you of it to force you to depend on Him alone, by abandoning yourself solely to His fatherly care. The more painful and violent your tribulation is, the better, I forecast, will it be for your salvation and your perfection. You will soon see this as I do.

Since Jesus Christ crucified is our only example, and since He wishes to save us by letting us be like Him, He sows crosses in the path to salvation for each one of us. If we are faithful these frustrations that cross our path will enrich us. And notice how great the mercifulness of the loving Saviour is. After having passed through the roughest tests and undergone the most painful sacrifices, the others begin to appear very light. O happy day, sweet in its fruits, harsh though they seemed at first!

LETTER 41

I am deeply moved by your account of your hardships, and above all of your sins and rebellion within. But, I know no other remedy than the one I have often recommended. Each time you experience a repetition of your misery humble yourself, offer everthing to God, and be patient. If you fall back into it, do not worry about it more than you did at first, but humble yourself more profoundly, and above all do not forget to offer God the pain within and the confusion which causes these revolts and sins, which come from your frailty. If new ones arise, always turn again to God with the same confidence, and endure as patiently as you can the new pangs of conscience and distressing inward resentment. As long as you do this, and struggle with yourself in this way, know that nothing will be lost. There will even be much to be gained by the unwished for rebellion that you suffer within. If a few faults escape, provided we try always to return to God and ourselves in the manner which has just been explained, it is impossible

93

not to make good progress. O how little sound virtue and true inward self-denial are recognized! If you learn once and for all to humble yourself sincerely for the least of your faults, regaining at once your peace by turning in confidence to God, you will make excellent and sure amends for the past, and a powerful safeguard and effective guarantee for the future.

I strongly approve of the dislike you have for argument. It is certain that in most of them there are illusions of self-esteem, because, as St Francis de Sales says, that wretched self-esteem interferes with everything, butts into everything and spoils everything. These are the effects of our pitiful human condition, to which we are always more or less exposed. When we recognize them in others we have two things to do: excuse those who have given in to them; and then ensure that we ourselves do not in turn become a subject of contempt to our neighbour.

LETTER 42

When anxiety causes us neither trouble, fear nor discouragement, it is as it should be. If it produces the opposite effect, it must be repressed and ignored, since then it surely comes from the devil or from pride, which is always unruly. In all our undertakings, even the most saintly, we must always wait peacefully on God, obedient and resigned to all His wishes. Why?

1. Because what God wishes and allows must alone rule all our own wishes, since all perfection consists in obeying and following continually every inward or outward circumstance in which we may find ourselves,

owing to the orders and promptings of that Divine Providence which extends over everything and rules everything down to the fall of a leaf or a hair of one's head, as Jesus Christ testified.

2. To abandon all our own wishes in order to submit them to God's, for which nothing is more appropriate than to give up our own good intentions. It is why God sometimes postpones His for a whole year or longer. It is then that we have a real need for faith, submission and confidence. And if occasionally we are afraid we have lost it, because the consciousness of our actions has been taken from us we must depend on the light of perfect faith and, by frequently turning to God to implore His help, humbly admit our helplessness, frailty, poverty and wretchedness. It is also to humble us and make us keenly aware of the need we have of His mercy, that God seems sometimes to leave us alone in order to show us what, deep down, we are really like.

3. O what a great favour and important advantage it is to have learnt by personal and frequent experience how much our frailty, our wretchedness, our poverty and our continual need of God's support enlightens us, encourages us, moves us and lifts us by the awareness of Grace within.

4. The inner strong conviction of a great longing to be stripped of your own wishes so as to have God's only, is one of His most precious gifts. In order to preserve and enrich it you must surrender your heart and your soul to it as often and for as long as possible. I would like you especially in your prayers to remain in that state all the time, in deep silence following the Spirit of God, unhur-

ried, calm and peaceful because God dwells only in a peaceful heart.

5. A strong mistrust of the world, with a strong desire to be wholly God's, are clear indications of the grace of Jesus Christ. If at certain times all that seems to you a fantasy, no doubt you will guard against falling for that temptation. You must then, as you do, surrender yourself more and more to all the commands of Divine Providence, who turns everything to the good and to the greatest advantage of those who live in complete abandonment and confidence, peace and tranquillity.

6. Inward uncertainties are trials sent by God which are equally just, holy, adorable, amiable and beneficial, whether they come from His justice or His mercy, and are usually partly one and partly the other.

7. I am delighted that the thought of your wretchedness and weakness, and the realization of your nothingness, is your usual inward preoccupation during your prayers. This is how, little by little, complete self-mistrust is acquired leaving not a scrap of confidence except in God alone. So also humility within, which is the firm and solid foundation of our spirituality and the mainspring from which God's Grace flows into the soul.

8. You must not be surprised or pained if you dread the loss of your self-esteem. It would not be self-esteem if you did not. Only saints already very much dead to themselves, far from dreading that complete death, long for it and ask God ceaselessly for it. For us, too, it is

sufficient calmly and patiently to endure all the various blows and attacks.

9. It often happens that we experience during the day certain feelings and an awareness of God and spiritual things which we do not have during our prayers. God does this to make us realize that He is master of His gifts and graces, giving them when He pleases and when we least expect them. Otherwise we should be tempted to imagine that they come partly from ourselves, our own aptitude, our own work and industry. But God has kept all the glory for Himself, in order that, through our futile complacency, we should not take any for ourselves.

3

Spiritual Poverty

God has truly granted you what you asked of Him in writing to me, because it seemed to me at first that I could read your soul, and that I knew it as though I had confessed and directed you for a long time. O what consoling and instructive things I have to tell you! I hope the Holy Spirit will make you understand and appreciate them, and that God will graciously give you His holy blessing in the name of Jesus Christ, the intercession of the Holy Mother of Joseph, St Francis de Sales and all his holy daughters, your sisters in heaven.

1. Your vocation seems to me to be marked with the stamp of God, with His divine will, His love, and His promise for eternity. Let us rejoice, bless God, and thank Him unceasingly for the great and precious gift of His grace.

2. The yearning God has given you to consecrate yourself to Him and for a life within, is, in spite of spiritual distractions and nature's rebellion, a secret grace. I would that it might please God to make you appreciate its value.

3. Why do you think, in spite of all this and all the holy books you have read, that you have remained at the

door, as it were, of the life within, without being able to enter it? Know, my dear sister and I see it very clearly, that it is because you have abused this impulse by your immoderate ambition, hurry and fervour, which displease God and extinguish the gentle action of Grace. It is also because there was in your conduct a secret and unconscious presumption which made you rely too much on your own initiative, industry and efforts. God has wanted to humble you and confuse you by your own devices, and so restrain your natural ardour which led you far beyond the sensations of Grace, as though you claimed to have achieved everything by your own efforts and even gone further than God wished, through spiritual ambition and love of your own progress on the spiritual highway. But console yourself, nothing is yet lost but rather much gained. God punishes you in this way tenderly like a good father, using that same punishment He calls trials, which He is accustomed to use in order to purify and free chosen souls whom He calls to perfect love and divine union.

4. That your dryness and suffering within have increased since you became religious I am in no way surprised, and I would have been very sorry for you if this had not happened. This is what we call continuation and increase of tribulation; a fresh assurance by God who intends in this way to raise up a soul to union with Him.

5. As for that continual distraction of which you complain so much, I believe, like you, that it is due partly to nature, a lively imagination and above all habit. But God has only allowed it in order to humiliate and confound you the more; and that in itself, causing you so

much distress, is part of the test: but it is by no means without remedy, nor is it the result of sin.

6. Your anxieties about this when praying are either temptations or pure fantasy, and God has been very merciful in disregarding them in spite of your false fears.

7. Your great fear and repugnance for everything external and for your employment: these are another part of the trial and greatly to your advantage in God's eyes.

8. Your acts of self-denial, sacrifice and abandon, are very sound and good in spite of the return of revolt within, which is again crucifying you. This is another part of your trial.

9. But the hardest, most difficult and most exacting part of the trial is the strong impression that God is rejecting you, and abandoning you as though He wanted to have nothing more to do with you. Ah my dear sister, how happy you would be if you understood, as I do, how that in itself is a loving act of God towards you! Everything I could say to you about that, although I doubt whether God would wish you to know it during your trials, is that never have you loved God so perfectly, but with a love so hidden in these trials and seeming misery that only experienced directors recognize it. But be patient, there will come a time of enlightenment and clarity which will enchant you.

10. O how I like it when you stand before God, like a dumb creature and overcome by temptations to deny faith and many other things! What more appropriate to humble, discontent and reduce to nothing a soul before

God! This is what He intends and where these apparent miseries lead to. Ah, if you knew then, in this humiliation, how to delight in maintaining an inward silence of respect and obedience for the love of God, to rejoice to see yourself as the plaything of His divine love! My God! How this silent respect within is renewed unconsciously from time to time simply by an obedient and contrite heart. My goodness! What an excellent self-sacrifice and what delight it will be to Almighty God! The sweetest and most fervent prayers, the most apparently heartfelt sacrifices, have no comparison and do not approach it.

11. Your worries about confession and holy Communion: another aspect of your trials, temptations and fantasies which must be rejected and ignored in order to go to God without anxiety, and to be patient about this as in all the rest.

12. As for the wish to avoid such an upheaval, that is pride and human nature crying out, the wish to rebel against the suffering of seeing ourselves pitilessly sacrificed. Then we must bravely resist this wish and hold fast to wanting only the fulfilment of the will of God in all things. This is essential, in order to soften the pains and see their end sooner. I even believe that they only last so long because you have not had the courage to make the sacrifices God wants you to by saying: "Yes, my Lord. I accept all, I submit to all, without reservation and for as long as you please."

13. What you add about your state of mind during prayer is a result of the trials and everything else. It would surprise me if it was not so. It may well be, my dear sister,

that you are wasting your time in prayer. You could make more tranquil ones, and may well do so later, if it pleases God, but you will never make any better, more useful or deserving ones, since prayers of the cross and suffering, being the most crucifying, are also those that are more purifying for the soul and bring about sooner the death of self, so as to live thereafter in and for God alone.

14. Those impressions of separation from God, which are so terrible in their effects, are what is called a work of the divine love, quite hidden, and crucifying so as to strip the soul of pride, just as gold is purified in a crucible by fire. O how fortunate you are without knowing it! How blessed without understanding it! How wonderful is the work of God within you, in a way more sure, the more obscure and unrecognized it is! It is our frailty, O my God, it is our wretched pride and arrogance which reduces You to granting us Your great mercies only by hiding them from us and, in a manner of speaking, unrealized by us, for fear that we should destroy Your gifts by accepting them with vain, secret and almost inperceptible complaisance. This is the whole mystery of this so hidden work of God.

15. From all this you will easily understand that you have only one thing to do. It is to let God do what He pleases and to remain inwardly in silence and peace, how and as much as you can. However, without struggling, gently and peacefully, so as to attain that unique goal which at present is your only need and which consists, I must repeat, in your total abandonment to God who controls. And in this peace and tranquillity within, in order to benefit fully from this divine operation and not to impede or disturb it, this is what you must do.

(a) You will go to your prayers to be tormented, afflicted and crucified as it may please God. When the dryness, temptations, disgust and anxiety overwhelm you, say to yourself: "Welcome, cross of my God! I accept you with a contrite heart, make me suffer so much that my pride is broken!" You will remain there before God like a beast overcome with its burden, and ready to succumb, but hoping for the Master's help and relief. If you are able to, throw yourself in spirit at the foot of the cross of Jesus, respectfully kissing His sacred wounds, humbly kneeling at His divine feet, firmly remaining there without moving, without doing anything else, but waiting quietly, and silently, like a poor wretch waiting for whole hours on end for alms at the door of a great king or a rich benefactor. But above all on no account should you think any longer of making any efforts, either in your prayers or elsewhere, to be more contemplative than God wishes.

(b) Concerning your daily prayers and the continual distractions which worry you, comfort yourself by recognizing that you do have a great longing to pray, but only when it pleases God, neither more nor less.

(c) If the distractions are sometimes so great, and dryness, tribulation, doubt and other grievances are sometimes so overwhelming that you are unable to make a single act of contrition or even to conceive a good thought, do not rebuke yourself. That is nothing. And all the better still if, in that deplorable predicament, you are able to maintain a respectful, submissive, and adoring silence within, of which I have often spoken. This should be your firm and continual practice in every circumstance. For therein lies your refuge, your shelter, where you only have quietly to try to make it your pleasure to see every wish of God accomplished in you, as though you could see Him up in the sky raining down on all the dryness, distractions, fears, anguish, and all kinds of miseries and humiliations, in order to make of you a plaything for His pleasure and divine love for you, somewhat as we see great princes rejoice and amuse themselves by splashing their favourites with mud.

(d) About the sacraments: guard against ever omitting either confession or communion. "But," you say, "if doubts and misgivings crowd in on me?" You must scorn and disregard them, and always turn to God without any arguing or reasoning for or against. Then, after having done quietly and without effort all that you could or knew what to do, rest in peace in that deep silence within of faith, respect, obedience and trust, of love and adoration, repeating often these words silently, "May my sovereign Lord and master do whatever pleases Him, Amen, Amen!"

(e) Since in all you tell me there is no sin, at least not any voluntary sin, although it may often seem that there is, remain tranquil and at peace, not in the lower part of your soul which is troubled and despairing, but in the upper part and high point of your soul, which can with God's help remain at peace in the middle of all the storms and buffetings. These are only, so to speak, on the outside of the soul and in the outward senses, so remain tranquil and at peace in order to crucify and make them die as is fitting, before being able to reach perfect love and union with God.

(f) Although I notice no sin in your behaviour, I find an ant-heap of faults and imperfections which could be exceedingly harmful without the following precautions. It is the anxieties, the unnecessary fears, the depressions, worries and despair which endlessly destroy your peace within, that are most essential, especially for you. "But what to do to avoid them?" you ask. You must do this: (1) Never give in willingly. (2) Never foster them or make any violent effort to strive against them, because that will redouble them. Drop them like one drops a stone into water. Think of other things, and talk to God about other things, as says St Francis de Sales. Then run back to your refuge, to silence within born of respect and obedience, of confidence and total abandon. "But if I sometimes make mistakes, even willing ones, about these things, what am I to do?" Again, you must do this: Guard against worrying about worry, troubling about being troubled, despairing about despairing, etc. But return immediately to God, not violently but humbly and gently and peacefully, even thanking Him that He has not allowed you to make greater faults. This sweet and gentle humility, together with confidence in divine love, will pacify and calm you within, which is at present your greatest spiritual need.

I forgot to tell you that your great longing for divine love,
in spite of the trials which followed, are in no way imagination or fantasy. Your longings are very real, very sound and very excellent. You must continue to have them, but let them be gentle and passive without ever giving way to their zeal and fantasies of the imagination or putting them into practice, which spoils everything.

What you experience during these longings and immediately after, in the feeling of wanting to retire into yourself which overtakes you, is nothing else but what I shall explain to you by making a comparison. When you throw a piece of dry and inflammable wood into a fire, it lights up slowly at first, without a sound. But if the wood is green the flame only lasts for an instant, and then the heat of the fire, acting on the green and damp wood, makes it ooze water, crackle and jump about in every direction very noisily, until in this way the wood becomes quite dry and ready to light up. Then the flame attaches itself, embraces it and slowly burns it gently and noiselessly.

That is an image of the operation and action of divine love in souls who are still filled with imperfections, bad temper and pride. They must be purged, purified and refined, and this cannot be done without agitating and making them suffer. See yourself, then, as that green wood on which divine love acts before being able to light up, embrace and consume it. Or like a statue in the hands of a sculptor, or like a stone which one cuts and shapes with hammer and knife to make it fit to be placed in a beautiful building. If that stone could feel, and if during its suffering it asked you: "My goodness, sister, what shall I do? I am suffering a great deal." You would no doubt reply: "Only remain firm and quiet under the hand of the workman, and don't interfere. Otherwise you will always remain a rough and shapeless stone." So take this advice yourself. Be patient and let God act, since, when all is said and done, that is all you can do. Only say, "I adore and I submit!"

The Feeling of Misery

LETTER 44

Nancy, 1734

My dear Sister,

The various states of mind which you describe in your letter are nothing more than the changing moods within to which we are all subject. This altering light and darkness, consolation and desolation, are useful and, I could add, as essential to the growth and ripening of virtue in our soul as the changes in the atmosphere are for the growth and ripening of the harvest in our fields. So, let us learn to be resigned and lovingly accept the trials as well as the consolations; because all these trials, even the most painful, are equally just, saintly, adorable, amiable and beneficent, whether they come from God's justice or His mercy. Often they come from both at the same time, although on earth justice never acts entirely separate from mercy. I am delighted that the thought of your misery, your weakness and the feeling of your nothingness should be your most usual internal preoccupation during your prayers. This is how, little by little, you acquire a total mistrust of self and gain a total trust in God alone. Furthermore, that is how we acquire humility within, which is the solid foundation of our spirituality, and the main source from which flow God's gifts into the soul.

You must not be surprised or pained that your pride is reluctant to be destroyed; it would not be pride otherwise. Only souls already very detached from themselves, far from fearing this total death, long for it and unceasingly pray God for it. For us, it is sufficient to endure silently and with patience the successive blows which it tends to create.

It often happens that at times we experience a certain feeling and relish for God and sacred matters which we do not have while praying. God does this because He wishes us to know that He is absolute master of His gifts and graces, that He gives them to souls as and when He pleases. Receiving them in this way when we are least expecting them, and seeing ourselves mistaken in this way, we can no longer persuade ourselves that they come from our disposition, our labour or our initiative. This is what God wishes. Because He is so generous with His gifts He claims all the glory for Himself. And He would be constrained to take them from us if He saw that we attributed them to ourselves, even though it were owing to our foolish self-satisfaction.

LETTER 45

Here are the causes of your distress:-

1. Ignorance of what your role in life is going to be, for some are easy and some are agonizing. With regard to people of the world, there are some whom God leads in the paths of prosperity, and others, but in much greater numbers, whom He leads in the stormy path of the cross, of afflictions and adversities. The work of salvation and perfection consists in marching faithfully, each one of us, along our path, following God's purpose for us whatever it may be.

2. Ignorance of that great principle that usually improves more by suffering than by action, and that is doing a great deal to know how both to suffer and to be patient at the same time, especially to have patience with ourselves.

3. Ignorance, in practice at least, is that perfection which does not consist of receiving great gifts from God, such as meditation, prayer, a spiritual taste for things that are divine, etc., but simply by adhering to all God's wishes in every imaginable circumstance, within or without, in which one could ever find oneself.

4. From this come those troubles, anxieties and despondency within, which have soured and redoubled your
despair, which have destroyed the peace of your soul
(which is the main foundation of the life within) and which
very often have led you to look for consolation from
humans, if only by telling them of your distress. God
wished you to look only to those He cares to give you,
when and how it pleases Him to do so. You must remedy
all that by other principles and quite different behaviour.

First Rule of Conduct

Repeat often to yourself: "My way is hard, and difficult it
is true. But such as it is, it is the will of God. It must be
obeyed, cost what it may."

(1) Because He is the almighty master who has the absolute
right to dispose to us as He pleases.

(2) Because He is our Father, with a heart so tender and
good, so merciful that He can only desire what is good and
best for His dear children, infallibly turning everything to
the advantage of those who are obedient and docile.

(3) Because I shall never find either peace or calm or rest in
my heart, or any true consolation, except by a humble and
patient acceptance of everything He arranges for me.

(4) Because I cannot advance one single step in the life
within except by following the path marked out and fixed
by the eternal decrees of my predestination. Could I make a
path myself, and if I could, would it not be like the path of
a blind man which leads to hell?

Second Rule of Conduct

I must wish for my advancement and perfection only in so far as and in the way God wishes. Otherwise it would be a wish stripped of its true excellence, arrogant, proud and imperfect. Consequently every wish, however holy it may seem, must be checked the moment bustle, anxiety and trouble appear which can only come from the devil. For everything that comes from God leaves peace and tranquillity within. Therefore, why wish with impatient eagerness for the light of the spirit, the feeling, the taste and the facility for meditation, prayer and all other gifts of God if He still does not wish to give them to me? This would be perfecting myself according to my wish and not His, and not according to having more regard for my liking than for His; in one word, wishing to satisfy my imagination and not to please Him.

But then, perhaps I would remain all my life in my poverty, my misery and frailty? But if that would please God, your suffering, misery and feebleness for that reason must be good and preferable to everything else, because God's will is to be found there. From then on that poverty is changed into wealth; because it is truly rich to wish only precisely what God wishes, in which consists supreme perfection. Besides, can you deny that there is a heroic virtue in knowing how to endure patiently and unceasingly one's misery, poverty within, gloom, insensitiveness, follies and extravagances of the spirit and the imagination? This is what made St Francis de Sales say that when we aspire to perfection we often have a greater need for patience, gentleness and support for ourselves than for others. Let us help ourselves, then, in our own miseries, imperfections and failures, as God wants us to help our neighbour in similar circumstances.

But, very often in this inward upheaval, the will suffers strange emotions and finds itself on the point of giving up and losing patience. Remain firm then – another occasion to combat victories, sacrifices, patience, triumph and glory!

"But if in the first moments that pitiful will has given in?" It must at once try to regain its composure, and quietly come, in sweet humility, before the Lord who is full of mercy.

"But all this orchestra within me distracts my attention during my prayers, during mass, in church, and during Holy Communion etc. And then all my acts of worship are lost?" Not at all, nothing is lost. The wish alone to complete what you have begun lasts and persists always unless you have cancelled it by a rather prolonged and quite conscious neglect. In a word, by a few sins quite deliberate and acknowledged. "And so, with all the merit of my spiritual exercises, I have in addition that of their having been exceedingly painful and tormenting and above all very humiliating. And therefore very far from spoiling those holy exercises by useless regrets and much self-satisfied pride." If they have given you any satisfaction, practise them with that blessed humility which is the foundation and guardian of every virtue.

"But this prevents me from feeling repentant." But true contrition is never felt; it is all purely spiritual, beyond the will. Conscious contrition is only food for pride and never reassuring because it is not the kind that God demands.

"But if I don't have it?" But you must believe and firmly hope that God has given it to you. When you have experienced it only once, the past sins having been already confessed, that is enough to restore everything, the past and present ones, so great is God's mercy.

Briefly, if it pleases God to make you realize your state of mind as I do, you would thank Him rather than distress yourself. Remain calm in every possible situation in which you find yourself. When you do that, everything is done. Repeat ceaselessly: "God be thanked for and in everything! I wish only what He wishes, no more. May all His very holy wishes be accomplished in me and by me. May none of my wishes be fulfilled. They are all blind and perverted. I am lost if they were to come true."

LETTER 46

You say you are never satisfied with your patience and submission in your suffering. Provided that discontent with yourself never becomes resentment, worry or discourage- ent, it will inspire in you a true and inward humility, a certain contempt for yourself which will be more pleasing to God and will do you more good than the most perfect patience and submission, which perhaps would only nourish your pride with secret and almost imperceptible self-satisfaction.

You say you still can only tell me of your misery. I can well understand it, because as long as we are in this world we can but find ourselves very imperfect and very miserable. But here is the general cure for us all. It is that, in hating sin, the cause of our misery, we like or at least accept the consequences; that is, our degradation and contempt of ourselves which result, all without worry, regret, anxiety or despair. For this reason, God, without wanting sin, nevertheless wants the results and the suffering, in order to foster our degradation and self-contempt which follow; without which we would certainly soon be overwhelmed by our thoughts. Believe me, remain content, steadfast and at peace in your sufferings, and try gently to diminish them. The more you do so, the more you will discover fresh ones. It is this increase of understanding that increases humility says Francis de Sales. But it must be a humility that is joyful and serene, loving our spiritual poverty, which then changes at once into true wealth. And know that it is beneath this dung-heap that God hides His gifts in order to rob them of the satisfaction of pride and our conceited self-esteem.

As for tears, when you shed them on account of your suffering, try to shed them in front of God and for Him. In this way, instead of bitterness, you will discover in them a secret balm which brings peace within through a total submission to all divine wishes. A submission which is the greatest good of reasonable human beings, though it may often be hidden in order to make the obedience more complete and more worthy. In a word, a strong sense of misery and our continual need of God's help is a great mercy which disposes of all good, especially prayers for humility and self-abasement before God, and confidence in submission to His infinite mercy, which is so pleasing to His divine majesty.

As for the imagined failure of your contrition, which distresses you: it is another temptation which robs you of peace. Well, don't you realize that the most apparently bitter repentance, accompanied by floods of tears, is neither the best nor a genuine contrition, nor one which God asks of you? In spite of that display we can still lack true repentance. On the other hand, without experiencing anything of that we can have a justifiable contrition of the will and heart which resides in the highest point of your soul. This is why perfect repentance is unconscious and purely spiritual. Rest, then, in peace, although pride requires you to feel and relish that repentance. God does not do so for many reasons, but chiefly in order to keep us always in that noble humility and in certain doubts which bring about our salvation.

So humble yourself profoundly then, and offer God in a spirit of contrition that vivid awareness of not having the necessary suffering. Sacrifice this suffering of your heart, by abandoning yourself totally to His mercy in the midst of the darkness and wholesome doubts through which He has resolved to lead us all, many as we are, not excepting the greatest saints, who, more faithful than we are, abandoned themselves totally to God and always remained peaceful because of their great trust in Him.

Concerning the examination of our conscience, when we make our usual confession, not out of necessity, but humbly and with devotion, each one of us makes it as we wish with the advice of our confessor. At the hour of our death we are not obliged to make a general confession. Nevertheless we must accuse ourselves of any grievous sins in a spirit of penitence and remorse, but without too much searching in order to spend the time in various acts of faith, hope, contrition, love of God, resignation, abandon, trust and union with the supreme sanctity of Jesus Christ. Moreover, the true preparation for death is the one we make each day by a good life in a spirit of meditation, self-abasement, self-denial, patience, charity, trust and submission.

When you talk to me of certain little precautions during illness, such as getting up a little later, warming one's bed, eating a little more at meals, these are mere trifles. Do what you feel and judge is necessary, with good sense, provided your concern within is in keeping with patience, obedience and total abandonment to God, and with a gentle and humble consideration for your neighbour. That is the essential, those are our saving virtues. People who are not very devout rarely miss outward things if only to make the most of them, leaving the enemy in his place, the enemy which is pride and human passion to which they do not wish to refer. But they have scruples of conscience about having eaten a few mouthfuls too many on a day of fasting. This is like the Jews, who make great scruples about going to Pilate, who was a Gentile, but none about the death of the Just One. And this is sometimes the case in religious people governed by similar illusions.

LETTER 47

My dear Sister,

Know that before curing you of vanity, God wishes to make you experience that evil passion in all its ugliness, together with your powerlessness to cure it, in order that all the glory of that cure shall be attributed to Him alone. And so you have only two things to do about this. First, to look on undisturbed by this frightful ugliness within. Second, to hope and await in the peace of God alone the moment for that cure, for which I am responsible at present.

You will never be at peace until you know how to distinguish what belongs to Him from what is your own.

You add in your letter: "Could you tell me the secret at once?" You don't know what you are saying. I can easily explain that secret in a moment, but you can only experience it within by having truly felt, and without resisting, all your suffering. I say "without resisting" in order to allow for the working of Grace. Here, then, is the great secret: not experiencing it all at once as you would like, in order to recover your perfection, as we put on a dress or a skirt, says St Francis de Sales; but in reflection, which little by little brings about what you hope for. Everything that is good comes from God, and everything that is bad, spoiled and corrupt, comes from you. So put aside the darkness, the sins, the bad habits and impulses, the abyss of misery, the weakness: that is your lot, and well and truly yours. All the rest – the body, with the senses, the soul with all its power, and the little pratical good – that is God's. And what so truly belongs to Him, you would not be able to take for your own the least thing without stealing it from God.

What you say within and so often, "Lord, have pity on me. You are all powerful", is best and simplest. You need nothing more to attract His powerful help. Hold fast to this practice and inclination within. God will do the rest without your perceiving it. I hope to see it come about in what follows. I am inwardly convinced that unless there is a great unfaithfulness on your part, God will bring about many things in you by His holy works. Count on this fully and don't consciously put any obstacle in the way. When by some misfortune you realize that you have done so, humble yourself at once and return to God and to yourself inwardly, always fully confident in His goodness.

The strong awareness of your misery and of the continual need of God's help is a great mercy, which disposes us to everything good, but above all to prayer, humility and selflessness before God, which pleases Him.

You do not understand, as I do, the working of Grace in

your soul. If you did you would be overjoyed. But your weakness and your lack of virtue do not allow you yet to endure it. The fruits of Grace still remain hidden as though buried in the abyss of your suffering under the deep consciousness of your weakness. It is beneath this dung-heap that God keeps all the fruits of His mercy. For such is the abyss of our suffering that we force God to hide from us His gifts and the wealth with which He enriches us within. Unless He did this, the slightest little puff of vanity and an imperceptible self-satisfaction would destroy or rot these flowers and fruits. When you are able to bear and rejoice in them without danger, God will open your eyes, and you will then do nothing but praise and bless Him, without once indulging in reflections on your conduct, attributing all the glory of your deliverance to your divine liberator. Meanwhile, follow the present guidance of His Holy Spirit and do not agitate your heart. Know that in all that is happening to you now, there is no sin, because you are suffering so much and you would be only too happy to be able to get rid of its agonizing effects. Foster these noble wishes, pray, and beg patiently, and above all humble yourself before God. It is for Him to complete the work He has begun in you. No one else could. Know that this is the difficult sacrifice God is asking of you before filling your heart with the ineffable delight of His perfect love. You will have no rest until this merciful intention has been realized, because your heart cannot exist without love. Let us pray, then, that this thirst will be quenched by the love of God alone, that it shall be Him and Him alone who charms our heart, who possesses it, sets it on fire, and enraptures it.

The abyss of misery and corruption in which it seems that God takes pleasure to see you submerged is, in my opinion, the grace of all graces, because it is the true foundation of all mistrust of oneself and total trust in God, which are the two opposite poles of the life within. At least of all the graces it is the one I prefer and the one I find more often in the best souls. What you think of yourself, then, however terrible, is nevertheless true and very well-founded, because if God left you to yourself you would become a mass of evil and a monster of iniquity. But God only reveals this great truth to a very few people, because few are capable of bearing it properly, that is to say peacefully, trusting in God alone, without worry or despair.

There is no other cure for habitual unfaithfulness than to suffer it, accept the humiliation and try to return to God as soon as possible. We shall suffer all our life from these punishments and humilities, because we shall always be ungrateful and faithless. But, provided it is only due to frailty of human nature without affecting the heart, that is enough because God knows our frailty, He knows what our suffering is and how incapable we are of avoiding infidelity. He sees even that He must reduce us to this state of misery, without which we could not repress the continual sallies of arrogance, presumption and secret confidence in ourselves. Guard against allowing yourself to be discouraged, although you see the failure of resolutions to turn to God so often renewed. Guard against despair, although you see the failure of the resolutions you so frequently make to belong to God. Use this repeated experience to fathom the deep abyss of your nothingness and corruption, so as to learn to mistrust yourself totally, in order to depend solely on God. Repeat often: "Lord, I will do nothing except what You make me do. Enlightened by a deadly experience, I no longer count on anything except the mighty power of Your Grace; and the more unworthy of it I am, the more hopeful I am, because my worthlessness makes your mercifulness shine." You will be able to have greater confidence in God. Infinite goodness and a mercifulness will produce infinite trust.

It is a very subtle and hidden illusion of pride to wish to know where we stand in relation to mystical death, under the pretext of being able to understand it as we should in order to make that death more complete in us. You will never know it in this life, and it is in no way an advantage for you to know it. Death itself, if it is conscious, runs the risk of no longer being death, because pride would be so pleased and satisfied of this assurance that it will revive and begin again to live a new life, more illusive and more difficult to destroy than at first. O God, how subtle is that miserable pride! It twists like a serpent and too often succeeds in preserving life in the midst of the most frightening deaths. That is the most specious of all illusions. Have a horror of that wicked pride. But know that, in spite of all your efforts, it will die once and for all in the last moment of your life.

The evidence of the sacredness of God which bewilders and mystifies you, without worrying you, is, in my opinion, a great mercy, more precious, more sure and more reassuring than previous consolation. Therefore I can only hope that it will continue. Make no resistance, allow yourself to be humbled, humiliated, debased. Nothing is better for purifying your soul and you will be able to bring to Holy Communion a mood more in keeping with the state of annihilation reduced in this mystery. He would not be able to reject you if you humbly approach Him, as though you were nothing, in the deep abyss of your misery.

When we have neither the spirit nor the ability to

discover our life within, after asking for mercy, we must remain still and silent. Your discouragement shows little purity of intention. This is a very dangerous temptation, because we must wish for no other improvement than to please God and not ourselves. And so we must be content with what God wishes or allows, because His will alone must be the rule and true limit of our wishes, even the most saintly. Moreover, we must never take it into our heads that we will reach a certain point where we will be satisfied with our self. This would be a great misfortune. The most certain indication of our improvement is to be convinced of our misery. In this way we shall be richer as we imagine that we are poorer, and we shall be more humble within, more mistrustful of ourselves and more disposed to confide in God alone. And that is what God is beginning to give you. And so: no anxiety, no discouragement!

I admire very much the practice you have adopted of not giving way to your feelings and of allowing yourself to be blamed and criticized, even in circumstances in which you consider you have good reason to justify yourself. You sacrificed, you say, that good opinion that you wished people had of you, and remained silent, even although, up until then, you had considered it better to defend yourself when what you said was correct. Here is my reply: Suffer silently all manner of blame and unjust accusations, without saying one word to justify yourself, under the pretext that what you said was in keeping with the spirit of the Gospel, and conformed to the examples of Jesus Christ and all the saints. Your ideas to the contrary were a pure illusion. Hold fast, then to your new and saintly conduct. You have reason to say that we carry a well of corruption inseparable from our nature, which is like muddy and infected water from which comes an insufferable smell when we stir it. This is a well-established truth, and God is doing you a great favour by making you see it so clearly. From this will be born, little by little, a noble hatred and total mistrust of yourself, in which true humility mainly consists.

LETTER 48

When you have neither desire nor inclination to read, simply try to remain quietly in the presence of God, and do not attempt to improve your life within until He gives you the knowledge, the impulse and the facility. Moreover, because in general you lack courage in many ways. Remain humbly willing, and regard yourself as not yet having done anything to allow you to hope in the mercy of God and the merits of Jesus Christ. That is the only reliable and true hope which totally annihilates and torments pride, leaving it no resources of its own, especially with respect to certain souls.

You say there are certain sacrifices that bring us to God, and others that turn us away from Him. This idea is an error and comes from judging what is good and what is bad more according to pious acts rather than to feeling. In certain sacrifices, which do not touch the heart where it is sensitive, we find an indescribable something which brings us perceptibly to God. But others which severely wound the heart only give us pain, worry, defeat and sadness. Furthermore, there is something else that is very agonizing, and that is the fear of suffering hardship without gaining anything from it. This is the source of the error that these sacrifices turn us away from God. Nevertheless it is a certain and sure principle that the sacrifices cost us and touch us on the raw. The more they make us die to self, to all consolation and palpable help, the nearer we approach and unite with God in a way which is more beneficial the more it is hidden, the more unrecognized and out of reach of the senses and all self-esteem, which cannot be sustained by what they cannot know or feel. God wishes to persuade you of so certain a truth by means of books and every experience.

For this you must know that there is in nearly all men such a depth of pride, frailty and wretchedness that they would not be able to recognize in themselves the gift of the grace of God, without debasing, spoiling or corrupting it by imperceptibly reverting to pride. It is what is called appropriating the gifts of God, to be pleased with oneself at being in such state of mind, which is the same as rewarding oneself not for any particular thoughts or reflections but for secrets of the heart, every corner of which is penetrated by God. Now, as God is and must be infinitely jealous of His glory which He cannot give to another, He must, in order to preserve it and to protect us from those secret thefts of the human heart, convince us by our own experience, of our infinite weakness, which is why He hides nearly all His gifts and graces in order to preserve them in us in their purity. I except, on the one hand, beginners, who need to be attracted and won over by these palpable and recognized gifts. On the other hand I except the great saints, who, having been purged of pride by hundreds of trials within, can recognize in themselves the gifts and Grace of God, without the least pride or indulgence in reflections on their own conduct.

Following this principle, I have constantly seen that God has so hidden His gifts and graces from most of the souls He has recommended to me, that they could see no progress in their patience, their humility, their submission and their love of God, that they wept at not having any of those virtues and not being able truly to suffer. But the more they worry and grieve themselves about it, the less the directors have to worry and grieve about them. You will understand this still better from what the illustrious Archbishop de Cambrai says about it. Here it is: "There is not any gift, however great it may be, which, after having been a means of progress, does not usually become a snare and a delusion of ownership which defiles the soul." It follows from this that God takes back what He has given, but not for ever. He takes it away in order the better to give it without the imperfection of this evil appropriation we make without realizing it. The loss of the gift serves to remove the ownership, which by being taken away, is returned a hundred times. All this seems to me to be so important to you that I think you should often re-read that long article, which alone can make you get over false prejudices and many other little errors that often trouble and spoil the peace within your soul, a peace without which we make scarcely any progress on the road to God.

I know someone very spiritual, and so well embued in this principle that I have heard her say many times that having asked for a long time and having made many novenas and prayers in order to obtain certain purely spiritual gifts, she often says to God: "I consent, Lord, to being deprived for ever of knowing if it has pleased you to grant me these gifts, because I am such a wretch that every known gift turns to poison in me, almost without my noticing or scarcely being able to avoid it. Such is the depth of my misery. This is how we ourselves, O my God, tie Your hands or force You to cancel, out of goodness, the gifts which in Your mercy You bring." You have, my dear sister, a greater need than hundreds of others for the same thoughts, for I have never known anyone who depended more than you on what is called moral support under the specious pretext of spiritual necessity. I have always thought, without mentioning it to you, that in the end the time will come when God, jealous of all support other than His, will remove them without your knowing or feeling in what way He will replace what He has taken away. This condition, I assure you, is terrible for human nature, but in that terrible flight, a simple *Fiat!* in all the bitterness and revolt in your heart, is a true and solid progress of the soul, in which there remains perfect faith in God. That is to say, an obscure faith, stripped of all conscious devoutness, but residing in the summit of the spirit, as St Francis de Sales says. Paul also assures us that we walk with God by faith: *Per fidem ambulamus.* We can easily understand those three words.

All this will convince you that it is no punishment but mercy, and a very great mercy, when God takes away more from you than from others. It is that He is more jealous of keeping all your heart and all its trust. That is why He had to take everything from you without making up for the deficiency in any way, even within the depth of your consciousness. For the rest, not so many reflections on present or future evils. Abandon, Submission, Love and Trust!

LETTER 49

I am sending you the book in question. It is a real treasure for you. I beg you to make it your customary reading in this manner:

1. By trying to grasp these comforting and lasting truths
   with common sense rather than with avid curiosity,
pausing now and again to let these sweet truths sink more
deeply into your soul and to make way for the work of the
Holy Spirit, who, during these quiet pauses and silent
waiting, engraves and imprints on our heart celestial
truths. All this, however, without disregarding your
inclinations, or doing anything violent to disturb your
reflections, but tending gently and quietly to savour
them rather than grasp them. Or, if you like, to penetrate
them with the promptings of the heart rather than the
conclusions of blind reason.

2. Mark certain more important chapters for which you
   have a greater need, so that you can re-read them at
your leisure some other time. With respect to occasions
when you suffer, let us try to make the most of the many
little opportunities which God gives us to conquer our
pride and that wicked vanity which becomes embittered
and irritated by everything, and causes us to make
thousands of faults, tearing us to pieces with disorder and
rebellion within.

As for an occasion of great suffering, we must continually believe that it will pass like all the rest, and that if,
when it happens it has passed and we are unable to get over
the fact that it has not benefited us, we must, as we say,
make a virtue out of necessity. To do this you must never
mention it except when it is necessary to do so, and then in
two words – that is to say, in as few as possible. Never
think of it or of the consequences consciously, but abandon
everything to Divine Providence, that will turn everything
to the greatest good and advantage of those who know
how to live by faith. I pray God that He will make you

understand those great spiritual and temporal rewards contained in the saintly practice of total obedience to all God's very holy wishes and to the gracious permission of His admirable and incomprehensible Providence, without whose orders – it is a fact of faith – not a hair of our head, not an autumn leaf from a tree in any forest throughout the world falls to the ground. Could Jesus Christ make us see more clearly than by these words that there is nothing so great or so small in the world that is not expressly obtained by that supreme Providence which extends over everything without exception? O my God! How comforting it is, when we learn how to see You, as You say, like a tender father, and You look on us as Your dear children, to whom You often give bitter but beneficial remedies. Have pity on those poor invalids, O infinitely merciful Father! On those invalids, who in their frenzy rebel against the charitable Physician and against the purge which will bring them health and life! O my God! How many blind and insane people there are in the world, who won't even hear these truths spoken of, although You have revealed them in Your sacred writings, only for our present consolation and our eternal salvation.

LETTER 50

1. I am overjoyed that God is making use of my letter to make you realize the immense difference there is between the feeling in the heart with regard to God and with regard to human beings. Here is the cure. After the great God's gift of Grace to you in giving you such a quick and profound understanding, there is no other way but to look on these miseries quite calmly, without resentment,

pride or arrogance. Because to endure all your suffering calmly and humbly (trying always, with God's mercy, to minimize them by untroubled vigilance and prayer) is, so to speak, in the eyes of God no longer to have them: that is a truth as lasting as it is hidden.

2. You need to consider often these words of our Lord to St Catherine of Sienna: "My daughter, I leave to all you human beings tender and sensitive love and prefer to reserve for myself love that is purely spiritual which resides in the high point of the soul, from which nevertheless everything inward is governed." According to St Francis de Sales, a loving mother who weeps and mourns the death of her dear children would not commit the most trivial sin even in order to bring them back to life. The same is true of contrition as of love of God. Everything takes place spiritually in the higher part of the soul and without our being conscious of it because, during this life, we are so wretched that every known gift turns to poison through our pride, which forces God, in some way, to hide His gifts. If we understood our interest properly, we would see this beneficent blindness as the most precious of all blessings. Like that saintly man Job, we would never kiss His hand more lovingly than when it seems to weigh most heavily on us.

LETTER 51

1. You agree with me that your restless eagerness is a fault, and you say that I would like to see you without faults and absolutely perfect. That is so. That has always been my wish for you. But this can only happen little by

little, by a great trust in God, who alone can complete the work He has begun. Submit yourself entirely to Him, leave all to Him. Do not be one of those who, as Jesus Christ told St Catherine of Sienna, makes little progress in perfection because they want to say and do everything without listening to Him or allowing Him to influence them.

2. I am overjoyed that you feel that God is visibly supporting you in your suffering. Remain as peaceful as you can, and in great calm and silence within. That alone will help you greatly to be still with God in your heart. He has given you courage – profit by that gift. At present the Divine Master asks of you gentleness and resignation in the depth of your soul and the high point of your spirit, without being aware of it. I can see that this is the way He has given you this gift and I thank Him for it. When, later on, this resignation becomes conscious it will fill you with the peace and serenity of some of the saints. It is then that you will taste the secret and heavenly unction which Jesus Christ attaches to participation in sharing His cross, in the marvellous effect of His Grace within. O what good fortune, what delight to discover peace and joy at the very foot of the cross! This is what brought unfailing peace and joy to the saints, and what, like them, people experience who aspire generously to a life within and perfection by sacrificing everything to God.

This life within, you say, seems impossible on account of your character and your temperament. In effect that is so, but what is impossible for man is easy for God. It is on Him alone that, through Jesus Christ, you must depend. This is why the Lord begins by making you so vividly aware of your weakness. But comfort yourself at once with hope, because God delights in seeing his Grace triumph over our greatest weakness.

May you so often repeat within: "Lord, have pity on me, You who can do all!" You need nothing more to attract his powerful help. Hold fast to this practice and right disposition of expecting nothing from yourself and continue to hope in God for everything. He will do the rest without your noticing, and I promise myself that I shall see it clearly in what follows.

I am inwardly convinced that, unless there is a great unfaithfulness on your part, God will do many things in you by His holy work. Cling firmly to that. Only try not to put any obstacles in the way wilfully through your own fault; and when you realize that you have accidentally done so, humble yourself at once and return to God and to yourself within, always full of trust in His divine goodness. We have only to attach ourselves to God and His holy will, acquiescing to all that follows which cannot but be fortunate and profitable, when on our part there is nothing but that blind submission to His orders, because it is in that that all perfection and the true love of God consists.

It is a great mercy to feel, as you do, the folly and absurdity of worldings, with regard to the things that please them. From this come great blessings to the soul. It strengthens the soul to depise the world and to live a life within. You will say that although you are scarcely yet there you esteem that state, you lean towards it, you admire it, you ask for it, you are on the way, you are walking towards it. These are so many various degrees of grace. The rest will follow in time. Nevertheless, moderate your spiritual zeal and your saintly ambition.

You are beginning, you say, to be somewhat indifferent to the good or bad behaviour of people towards you. This is a greater mercy than you think. There are still times of sadness and despair which seem stronger than yourself, you say. Then you must endure them as best you can, especially the pain of seeing and feeling oneself so feeble. This is what most hurts our spiritual pride which is revolted by the sight of our failure, our wretchedness, our frailty and powerlessness. This is also the greatest and most humbling sacrifice, from which, with St Francis de Sales, I conclude that we, more than others, have need to be patient and tolerant of ourselves.

It is quite permissible to wish for some sympathetic and even visible help or support on our path to God. But it must be wished for in moderation. Seek it without too much eagerness, using it without depending on it, accepting it when God wishes. I don't say without pain, trouble, despair; without apparent and expressed regret, or anxiety. And failing all else, hope in God; turn from time to time and for everything to God, down to the most trivial needs, as little children turn to their dear mother. That saintly simplicity, that humble and childlike conduct towards God, touches and charms His fatherly heart, and we receive, sooner or later, everything we ask of Him; or something even better, which is often given to us without our being able even to understand it.

What our Lord said to St Catherine of Sienna, that men wish to do and say so much that they don't give Him the chance to operate in them, must be understood as that when we are busily accomplishing our duties, we do so without too much bustle nor with a kind of human hurry and impetuosity. And that, during the day, we are, so to speak, listening to Divine Wisdom within, in order to hear Him who is speaking in the depth of our heart, voiceless, without syllables, because His word is His work. Moreover, that in all our prayers, reading, self-examination, elevations to God, etc., all is done gently, mildly, without confusion, without effort, seeking only peace of heart in God, and for this allowing frequent pauses to make way for God to operate freely and at His leisure in our souls, as and how He pleases.

What you tell me about your fears that faults may be made more grievous by the presence of God, are illusions of the devil, who tries in this way to discourage you from your adherence to that Divine Providence and from taking the sacraments regularly. Continue both these exercises without anxiety. I see their fruits, and they will become so evident that in time you will see them for yourself.

I congratulate you that God has taken from you some of the impetuosity of your nature. As for your gaiety, it will only be gone for a while, it will return, but entirely changed, or rather transformed into a spiritual joy; tender, serene and peaceful because it will be like that of the saints, entirely in God and coming only from God.

I approve your way of praying. Continue in the same way, pray when you have a gentle inclination to do so. When, during pauses and silence within, good thoughts and ideas come to you, receive them calmly, and the same with inward tranquillity, now greater, now less, as it may please God. In a word, wait always on almighty God, more with the heart and in your desires than consciously in the head. And always be content with whatever you are given. God knows better than we do what we need. Leave it to Him. Only let us always be convinced that the least peace in the heart and in His holy presence is worth more than anything we could say or think. May this conviction induce you always to allow the heart this holy rest and not to interrupt when God gives it, for these are preciois moments of intimacy.

My dear Sister,

You must submit to God in and for all things – for the condition and the circumstances in which He has placed us, for the benefits and hardships He has dealt us, and even for the character, spirit, nature, temperament and inclinations with which He has endowed us. Practise patience with regard to yourself, and to that perfect submission to the divine will. As soon as you have acquired it you will enjoy great peace, no longer grieving about anything, not despising yourself, but tolerating yourself with the same gentleness which you must show to others. This is more important than you think. And at this moment perhaps there is nothing more essential for your sanctification. So, keep this always in mind and make frequent acts of submission to the holy will of God, of love, of tolerance, gentleness for yourself and for others. You will not achieve this without doing great violence to yourself.

A soul to whom God makes known its wretchedness is a much greater burden to herself than her neighbour could ever be; because, however close he may be, he is not always near us. In any case he is not in us, whereas we carry ourselves, and we can never leave ourselves for one instant, nor cease completely to see ourselves, to be conscious of ourselves and to drag our imperfections and faults around with us everywhere. But here is when the infinite goodness of our God is especially revealed to us. It is that suffering and shame of which these faults are themselves the cure, always providing that this shame does not turn to malice and that the suffering was inspired by love for God and not by our pride. Suffering which derives from pride is full of trouble and bitterness, and far from healing the wounds in our soul they serve only to make them worse. On the other hand, love for God is serene and full of submission. If it detests the sin, it delights in the humiliation that follows. Thereby the loss is changed to gain and the humiliation given its full deserts.

Cease tormenting yourself on account of your short-comings. Offer God the anguish they cause you, and let merciful Providence repair that trivial faithlessness by all kinds of little trials and tribulations. Arm yourself only with patience, recover yourself as soon as you can; never groan over your fall except in sweet and tranquil humility. That is how God wishes it to be. And by that tireless patience you give Him more glory and make more progress than you could ever do by making more violent efforts.

Doubts and Scruples

LETTER 53

If you wish, my dear sister, a fragment of faith will be sufficient for ever to free you of the doubts which torment you with regard to your confessions. For this you have only to follow the infallible rules which I am going to lay down for you.

1. Never ask to be relieved of that torment, because God has quite clearly made you feel why He has allowed it.

It is because He alone wishes to be your total support, consolation and reassurance, without destroying the purity of your love. Not finding in you the courage which led the saints to that perfect purity by heroic sacrifices, He leads you gradually by less agonizing tests. Thank Him for His condescension, and do your best to respond to His merciful intentions.

2. Henceforth, here is how to prepare for your confessions. After at the most a quarter of an hour of examining your conscience as best you can, you will say to yourself: "By God's mercy, I live in continual contrition, because I would not commit a mortal sin for anything in the world. I feel the same horror for venial sins, although I do unfortunately still commit them. And so there is nothing else for me to do, therefore, but to make an act of thanksgiving as best I can, for the inclination God has put in my heart in His great mercy." Not much time is needed for this, a few minutes suffice. And the best way of bringing about acts of contrition is to pray God to bring them about in us Himself.

3. "But", you will say, "if I find it impossible to remember any fault clearly how will I be able to make my confession?" This is what you will say, "Father, my lack of understanding prevents me from recognizing my daily faults. But I come to accuse myself in general of all the sins of my past life, and in particular such and such a sin, for which I beg God's forgiveness with all my heart." After that, you will accept unprotestingly the patience your director imposes upon you, and you must not in any way doubt that the absolution he pronounces on you will not confer all the gift of grace that goes with the sacrament.

Is there anything else in the world, I wonder, easier and more consoling? And if you adopt this practice, will you not in the same way be delivered of the suffering which has so greatly tormented you to this day?

I shall hope that this modest act will become known and practised by many members of your community, who are experiencing the same difficulties as you are, and who, like you, could easily overcome them.

Dryness and Darkness

LETTER 54

Take courage, my dear sister, and do not persuade yourself that you are estranged from God. On the contrary, never before have you been closer to Him. Remember the agony of our Saviour in the garden of olives, and you will understand that bitterness of heart and violent anguish are not incompatible with perfect submission. It is the groan of suffering human nature, and an indication of the hardship of the sacrifice. And so do nothing against God's orders. Say not a word of complaint or self-pity. That is the perfect obedience born of love – the most perfect love. Oh, if in similar circumstances you knew that you should say nothing and do nothing, but maintain a silence of faith, adoration, submission, abandon and sacrifice, you would have discovered the great secret of sanctifying and even alleviating all your suffering. You must practise this, gradually shaping up to it, being careful not to give in to worry and despair when you fail, but returning immdediately to that deep silence with calm and untroubled humility.

LETTER 55

Since you try to abandon your worldly affairs to Divine Providence, but taking, nevertheless, some care not to tempt God, do the same for your spiritual advancement, and without neglecting the care. Leave all in the hands of God, hoping for nothing except from Him. But never dwell on these diabolical thoughts: "I am always the same, always as miserable, as uncontemplative, as dissipated, as impatient, as imperfect, etc." All that trouble within overwhelms the heart, plunges you into sorrow, mistrust, and despair, and that is what the devil intends by that would-be humility and regret for one's faults. Rely on yourself meekly, gently turn to God, quietly repenting – not too vehemently inwardly or outwardly, but quietly. This alone, well carried out, will gradually bring you calm within which will advance you in the ways of God more than anything else you could do. Because, when we feel peace and rest in our heart, we return to it with pleasure, and what we do with pleasure, we do willingly, continually, painlessly and almost without thinking. For your support, believe me, put all your trust in God through Jesus Christ. Depend evermore totally on Him in and for everything, and you will discover by your own experience that He will always, without fail, assist you when it is necessary. He will make Himself your master, your guide, your stay, your protector, your invincible support. Then you will lack nothing, because whoever has God has everything, and in order to have Him you have only to go to Him with complete trust, in and for everything, great and small, without exception. And always say to God:

"Lord, what shall I do in such and such a circumstance? I abandon myself totally to You. Enlighten me, guide me, uphold me, possess me."

I sympathize with the worry and difficulties you tell me about. But remember that it is only patience and obedience within that will help you more than the most serene and most contemplative life. Because that always flatters our pride a little, whereas the other torments and crucifies it. And this is what destroys that wretched love of self, and which brings true peace in the heart through union with God.

When you find yourself in such heartfelt depression that you are unable to make a single act of prayer about anything whatever, be careful then not to torment and struggle with yourself, but come to God in silence and prostrate with respect, humility and submission, like a criminal before his king and judge who gives him the punishment he deserves. And know that silent prostration and submission within are worth more, and purify the heart sooner, than all the useless acts of penance we attempt to make, and which often agitate the soul even further.

The character you describe of that person is excellent. But to hate your own for that reason, that is not good. You should, with submission and respect for God's command, wish to be as He wishes us to be, without however neglecting to reform yourself. Now, the best and essential reform I should like to see in you, would be never to embitter your heart for whatever reason, but always to treat yourself with the same gentleness that you would show to a neighbour, about whose character you would not make sour remarks but whom you would gently try to reform. Do the same with regard to yourself, and if gradually this spirit of gentleness can fill your heart, you will soon make progress in your spiritual life without so much difficulty. But if the heart is easily filled with rancour and bitterness, we make little progress with great cost. I stress this point, I would apply myself to acquiring in everything an inward and outward gentleness of spirit. As there is no other virtue to acquire, you will find that this one will lead you to all the others as soon as you have practised it quite calmly for a short time, without giving way to fervour and haste which seperate you from that very gentleness you wish to achieve.

LETTER 56

1738

1. As to your first point, quite definitely you must totally abandon yourself to God without reservations, without limits, without end. He asks this of you, do not doubt it. Your great mistake, and also your great grief up to the present, is to imagine that you lack the good will which God always demands. Yes, certainly, a conscious and recognized willingness; but there is a fundamental good will which God reserves in the depth of the soul, which I know very well to be in you, despite all your feelings to the contrary. Therefore, be comforted by what I say, and firmly believe that this depth of good will remains imperceptibly always in you as a quite unique result of the grace of Jesus Christ, and your abandonment itself greatly helps to perfect and increase that good will, hidden though it may seem to you. This is a certainty, firmly believe it, and in the end your own experience will confirm it.

2. The limitations of your willingness is a great weakness in you, as it is in many others. Why? Because you try to come to God by recognized acts of faith of your own choice. God does not wish it, and you are greatly to blame for attempting to do so. It is an unfaithfulness which will cost you dearly. What is to be done, then? What you can do is something for which the power is never lacking, and that is the one simple desire which God perceives in all your acts which you wish to do for your own satisfaction or self-confidence. But God does not wish this, in order to make way for a more perfect abandon. And so, cease to be distressed or to grieve and lament over your genuine weakness. Then say *Fiat! Fiat!* That is worth infinitely more than all you could wish to say or do in your own fashion, according to your own ideas and your own judgement. I allow you, however, on account of your frailty, to say to yourself from time to time: "I know that although I normally long to turn to God I find I am unable to do so." But does God not see this wish? And this wish alone tells Him all, even though it is immediately stifled or checked. But, you will say, it sometimes seems to me that I lack this wish. And I say to you then, why does this supposed lack give you so much worry? — for we only worry about the lack of something in proportion to how great our wish for it is. If we have no wish we have no wish to worry about. You are not so very greatly troubled at not having riches, honours and beauty. That is because these thinks no longer mean anything to you and you simply don't think about them.

3. You are experiencing a great scarcity of grace and strength because at present God wants nothing from you. But you have no scarcity of holy desires, and being

unable to carry them out causes you so much anguish. Remain, therefore, at peace in your great spiritual poverty, which is a true treasure when one knows to accept it willingly for the love of God and because He wishes it. It is a matter of faith that everything, except sin alone, is God's will. I can see quite well that you have never understood true poverty and barrenness of spirit, whereby God succeeds in detaching us from self and our own achievements, in order the better to purify us, simplify us and limit us to acts of pure faith and spirituality, a frame of mind which is the last step to our perfect union with God. It is true that this is a real death to self, a death which is very deep, very agonizing and very hard to bear. But it is only by this inward torment that we die to all self in order to live only in God, and of God, through Jesus Christ and with Jesus Christ. Understand your blindness here, in lamenting your spiritual advancement as you do, which after a certain progress is and can only be achieved through deprivation, barrenness, annihilation, and death of body and spirit, in order to unite immediately with God, which one cannot feel, recognize or prove. O daughter of little faith, intelligence or courage, who torments and drives herself to despair by what should console and rejoice her! Tell yourself-love to despair as much as it wishes to see itself dying so completely, but your soul will rejoice in God at its despair, even though it were to die of vexation.

4. Is it possible that this powerful yearning to belong entirely to God, and a moment after to feel yourself repulsed by an all-powerful hand, gives you a feeling of despair and a sense of being censured? Whereas that in itself should make you feel quite differently, because these two contrary states of mind are an infallible sign of the

most precious working of the Holy Spirit to bring about in you, by this inward crucifixion, the most complete death of self? But what can I say? If God lets you understand it, as He does me, this trial will cease to be one and will change into unutterable joy. Happy girl, without knowing it. Why double your pain uselessly with thoughts quite contrary to those of God?

5. But what shall I do, you will say, when I am unable even to make a token submission? Submit to that submission itself with a simple *Fiat!* It will then become the most perfect submission. Forgetting God, you say, seems to you hell. Oh what a grand sentiment, which charms the heart of God and which comprises the most perfect act of love! Profane lovers sometimes go as far as that in extravagant love. It is your sense of deprivation and sacrifice which have led you to that saint-like immoderate and desperate love. It is precisely this inward deprivation, anguish and impotence that is God's purpose.

6. God almost always allows these kind of torments to seem to the soul to have no ending. Why? To give it the opportunity to abandon itself more completely, indefinitely, without limits and without restraint, in which consists pure and perfect love.

7. Once again, you are powerless to do what God does not wish you to do, and which it would not be expedient for you to do. But God works in you, with you and through you something so excellent that, if you understood it, you would go on your knees to thank Him for some of the weaknesses which prevent interference by your miserable and pitiful actions in the purpose of the

141

Holy Spirit working in you almost secretly, but which I notice quite clearly and for which I give thanks to God for you, poor blind soul that you are.

8. There is no need to explain your difficulties and doubts. These are no sins, but purely crosses within, and it is only a question of enduring them with unbounded submission. It also is why God has made you so powerless to speak about them for so long or to think about them clearly, because nothing sanctifies the hardships we suffer as much as silence without and within. O what a great offering the *Fiat!* then is, especially if it is hidden in a simple wish that we can scarcely distinguish, but in which God perceives all the magnitude and extent of that same offering, all that we hope to tell Him without having the least consolation or assurance, which wounds our pride and plunges the soul into veritable agony.

LETTER 57

Great suffering disheartens everyone. One only recovers by trusting God and submitting to His Divine Providence. And when it seems that we are unable to do so truly, but only half-heartedly, we must submit ourselves in that too to the divine will, always with meek and patient humility. Because God only allows us to be overcome by this impotence and despair in order to make us recognize and feel more clearly our suffering, so that not a scrap of self-confidence remains in us, but only in Him alone and in His almighty grace. About this I must tell you that I have for a long time noticed in you one great gift of grace which you never consider. It is that you appear to me to be deeply penetrated by your wretchedness, frailty, faults and imperfections. Now, this only happens in so far as God draws near to us and we live and walk in His light, who, without any consciousness on our part, makes us see and feel, recognize and perceive an abyss of misery and corruption inside ourselves. This is one of the clearest indications of our progress on the way to God and the life within. And this is something for which you have never thought to give thanks! There is nothing left now but to try to live in peace by conforming to divine will amid this abyss of wretchedness and impotence. If you were able even to love this saintlike humility, the contempt and disgust for yourself which arises out of such an attempt would be an even greater step in your spiritual progress. So, recognize God's goodness in wishing to enrich you by the sight of your poverty, well loved, accepted and cherished because He wishes it so. Not, however, forgetting the wish to improve; for we must always join to the realization and hatred of our faults the wish and the care to cure them.

The pressure of work, the demands and worries of your worldly existence, in the view of Divine Providence that allows them, are well worth gentle meditation and silence. It is a kind of continual prayer of patience, endurance and resignation. But aren't we sometimes impatient? Well, this is the fascination of that prayer. One tries to recover at once and to calm oneself, because it is God who allows what is making us suffer. However, one cannot control being impatient about being impatient, or being anxious about being anxious. One meekly humbles oneself, and by that alone gains more than one has lost.

I don't need to go into detail on the subject of this sharp and sensitive pain which you tell me about. I understand all the diverse and cruel thoughts which are turning over in your mind, and all your heartbreak. But, my God, my dear sister, what an opportunity if you knew how to take advantage of it! Do this: (1) Pray frequently for the person who has caused you this unhappiness. (2) Keep a profound silence, not speaking to anyone to relieve your feelings. (3) Don't dwell on them wilfully, but divert your mind to other holy and useful thoughts. (4) Watch over your heart so that it does not indulge in the least bit in bitterness, spite, and wilful murmurs and revolts. (5) Try, at whatever cost, to speak good of that person. Look on her face with a friendly eye, behave towards her as if nothing had happened, except that she can no longer be treated with the same confidence and intimacy unless one is a saint, which you are not yet. (6) Be kind and help her on all occastions, and wish her the best of everthing.

LETTER 58

1. I have only one word to say to you about that heavy and painful burden which weighs always on your heart; a straightforward acceptance. A humble *Fiat!* of which you are scarcely aware, but which God operates and sees very clearly in you, can alone save you and make of you a martyr to His Providence. Besides, you will never believe how many good deeds are included in that feeling of being overwhelmed which is the cause of that great heaviness of heart, which is a greater mercy than you imagine. It is what is called the true penitence of the heart, which God has made you feel at certain times. Say to Him often that His holy will will always be the rule and measure of your most saintlike and beneficent desires, wishing only

144

for the degree of virtue and eternal happiness He has resolved to give you.

2. Go to Communion as often as you are allowed to, and submit meekly and obediently to all the suffering this entails. The best frame of mind and the most rewarding is to maintain yourself courageously and submissively along the path that God is leading you.

3. Your hardship, and the way of life you are reduced to, is an excellent penance, and the best you can offer. And yet you are afraid that you are deluding yourself by not fasting in this suffering state of mind! Vain fear! Obey the doctor blindly. God requires it of you. Offer Him your pain as often as you can its hardships, and fears, in the heart only, quietly remembering to wish for what God wants. Just the thought and a look towards Him is enough.

4. The comparison of your hardships and those of others is very reasonable and very Christian. God also gives it His benediction by the good effect these saintlike comparisons have on you.

4

Father de Caussade's "Abandon"
(Perpignan 1740)

1. What I have always apprehended has happened to me. In spite of my groaning, praying, begging, offering to remain all my life in the novitiate of Toulouse, the greatest sacrifice of my life had to be made. But here is where adorable Providence becomes visibly apparent. This sacrifice made and repeated a hundred times, God has removed from my heart all my old dislikes, so that I left the monastery, which you know that I so loved, with a kind of peace and freedom of spirit, at which I myself was astonished. There is more to tell. That is, on arrival I found many temporal matters of which I understood nothing; many people to see and to deal with: the Bishop, the King's representatives, Parliament's representatives, state officials, and so on. You know my horror for all sorts of visits, and especially from the great. But nothing of that frightens me. I hope that God will remedy all that and I feel a confidence in His Divine Providence, which helps me to rise above it all, providing I remain calm and tranquil through various cares and difficulties which I would normally have expected to overwhelm me. It is true that what most contributes to this great peacefulness is the disposition which God has given me not to fear or expect anything from this short and miserable life. And so, when I have done the things I think I should have done before

146

God, the result will please Him. I have abandoned them wholly to Him with all my heart, blessing Him in advance for everything, wishing only for His holy will in everything and everywhere, because I am convinced by faith and many personal experiences that everything comes from God and that He is powerful enough and too good a Father not to make everything turn out to the greatest advantage of His dear children, whom He loves more than His life, since He sacrificed it for love of them.

2. I am very afraid that your eagerness may disturb your peace within. Don't you know that as soon as I have done something before and according to God, I leave all the care and outcome to Him, following quietly in step with His Divine Providence that rules and arranges everything for our greatest good, even though usually we neither know nor are aware of it, poor blind and ignorant wretches that we are, like the moles who live under the earth.

3. Let us accept everything at the hand of our loving Father, and He will keep us in peace through the most terrible disasters in the world, which pass like a flash of lightning. In proportion to that abandon and total confidence in God, we shall lead a saintlike and peaceful life; but furthermore, without that (at least to a certain extent) there is no true virtue, no certain peace.

4. You were wrong to be surprised that I was not in agreement with the projects of N., and besides the fact that nothing surprises me in this life, you must know my way of looking on the bright and most favourable side of everything, as says St Francis de Sales. This fortunate habit

puts me out of the risk of evil thinking, evil judging, evil talking about anyone, whoever it may be, and contributes greatly to the peace of the soul and purity of consciousness. Let us sacrifice human considerations, and console ourselves with obedience to and trust in God alone, because He alone is able to, and must, take the place of everything for us. Tell the dear Sister when you next see her that I say the same to her. I wish her, as I do you, eternal riches.

LETTER 60

Your great desire to . . . is excellent, but you must see to it that it is always submissive and resigned and as a result always peaceful, since, as you know, in your most noble desires nature and passion are always mixed and then they become violent, restless, apprehensive, impatient and turbulent. It is also in order gradually to purify our most saintlike desires, that God often does not fulfil them for a long time, because nature's unruly wishes do not deserve to be fulfilled. Only those inspired by the Holy Spirit, and which are always gentle, serene and peaceful, deserve to be granted by God. Remain at peace as much as you can, and even in a saintlike joy in order to be able to profit from all the beneficial impressions of good which penetrate so much more a joyful and contented heart.

It is true that at first all my present circumstances caused me a great deal of pain, being so contrary to my preference for silence and solitude. But this is what Providence has provided. God has been merciful to me by detaching me from all these things, and so my spirit is always free; I leave their success to His fatherly care, which means that nothing vexes me. Often things go as I hoped for, and then

I thank God. Sometimes everything goes wrong, for which I still thank Him and offer the troubles to Him, and that done, God repairs everything, which is an agreeable surprise.

As for time to myself, I have more than anywhere else. Visits are rare at present, because I only make them out of duty or necessity. Our fathers themselves, who know my preference, soon have done with me and I with them. And since they are persuaded that it is neither out of pride nor dislike, no one disapproves of my conduct and many are edified by it.

Moreover I am not so dead as you imagine, but God mercifully has allowed me not to worry about making enemies by following His way. It is Him alone that it is to our interest to please. Provided He is pleased that is enough, all the rest is nothing. In a few days we shall come before that almighty God, that eternal Being. Alas, what will they profit us then or for all enternity, those things not done for Him, nor quickened by His grace and by His spirit? If we yielded to these simple and quite familiar truths, what peace of heart and mind would we not enjoy from now on? From how many vain doubts, vain desires, vain anxieties would we not free ourselves for this life and the next? I assure you that, since my return to France, I begin to look forward more than ever to the end of this sad life, and this with a great peace and serenity, and with more honest longings to see the end of my pilgrimage close at hand.

You are right when you say that if you were to be rid of your present affliction you would become wholly decadent within. Nothing is more true. Affliction summons us back to God, unites us to God, makes us respect, fear and love God. The despicable revolts of human nature also have a good effect, which is to keep us very lowly and humiliated before God and in our own spirit, with a very low opinion of ourselves. Therein consists true humility within which makes us truly despise ourselves, and which preserves and safeguards all other virtues.

If what God makes you feel about your suffering and become aware of it makes you stand in awe of Him untroubled and growing in confidence, that is one of His greatest gifts of grace. But if that sadness and that humiliating awareness troubles, disturbs and tortures you, it is a great imperfection. Try to overcome it by remaining at peace, sincerely acknowledging your frailty and not wishing for any other support, help or hope than in the infinite goodness of God and in the power of Jesus Christ, never being thankful for anything, or attributing anything to yourself so as to owe everything to God and His divine Son, your Redeemer. Try to put all your inward trust in that righteous sentiment, "Others will have done a great deal for God, and I, having done nothing or scarcely nothing, wish to be indebted to all His perfect love and that is my only resource in all my suffering." Nevertheless, strive always to seize the opportunity to diminish and overcome them courageously.

The condition of P.T. is worthy of pity. God truly wishes to save him, since He inflicts so much suffering on him at the end of his days, at a time when it is very hard for human beings to be neglected. But how consoling to suffer greatly for God before going to God and standing before Him! Having a burden to be relieved of, like N., is truly a gift from God, but very different from the other. God protect me from similar gifts. I might grow to like them and put my trust in them. Mediocre virtue may well profit from the first gift, but it takes a heroic virtue, according to God, to profit by the second.

I am yours in our Lord until death and even after, if God is merciful, as I greatly hope He is.

LETTER 61

1. Since you find my letters so consoling and useful I promise you that wherever I might find myself, I will reply promptly.

2. Our inadequate knowledge and even our misjudgement of total submission to the will of God in all things does not rule out the essential truth and merit of a certain basic submission. It is sufficient to humble oneself and repair these errors as soon as one can.

3. I understand, better than you imagine, your permanent heartache and the burden which seems to overwhelm it. I have been in the same state for many years, and for a far less important reason than yours, which drove my inward pride to despair. I made many mistakes, but tried immediately to retrieve them. It was not until some time after this test that I recognized its advantages, which subsequently seemed to me so great and so numerous that, even today, I thank God for having stricken me, not with His justice but in His mercifulness, in making me go through that purgatory within. I feel sure that, in His time, God will bring you round to the same view, and that you will never tire of thanking Him for the afflictions which you are suffering today.

4. Similarly I have experienced, on I don't know how many occasions, that same redoubling of pain like a fever. Just as in the most serious illnesses there is nothing to do except try to remain silent within and at peace, as far as one can. As for intentional prayers, one is scarcely in a condition to make them then; at least, none that are reasonable and comforting. But God sees the basic submission or the longing for it, which always remains in the heart, and that is sufficient for spiritual merit and advancement, all the more so when without any consolation.

5. It is not forbidden to ask God for the pain to cease, especially when it acutely assails our heart. This it is what Jesus Christ did in the garden of olives. But it it necessary to add, as He did, "Your will be done and not mine". And although one adds these words reluctantly and with great distaste and much inward resentment, what does it matter, because it is our inferior side that is fighting, resisting and fretting. Nevertheless it is more and more necessary to submit, however vexing it may be, and it is that which makes our inward spiritual merit and advancement.

6. It is quite right that you should be made to take the sacraments as usual. Your greatest mistake would be not to, which would do you a great deal of harm. Neither inward depression, shame, nor embarrassment should ever draw you away from Holy Communion. These sad feelings suffered and accepted for God are worth more than palpable delight, ardour and comfort, which only nourish and foster our sensitive spiritual pride, while the other feelings serve little by little to make it die. And it is in this

depth that true piety and all spiritual progress consists, without which the most devout people's devotion is only on the surface.

7. As for your unsettled health: another daily sacrifice! You must subject yourself to the treatment and even to the sad necessity of not fasting if that is ordered. Your reluctance or your scruples on that account have no foundation. You must sacrifice these afflictions and your seemingly spiritual reluctance. The contrary would be a real illusion, to which I have seen many deluded people given, even the religious under the pious pretext of devoutness. It is surprising that the devil attacks such feebleness, it makes no sense.

LETTER 62

Your incurable, or scarcely curable, ailments would touch me with great compassion if I did not know for certain that for you it is a great treasure for eternity. It is a kind of martyrdom or purgatory, an inexhaustible source of all kinds of sacrifices and continual acts of submission. I assure you that, if they are endured, as they are in your case, without complaining or grumbling and with just the normal patience of every good Christian of natural indignation, notwithstanding a few moments of impatience which escape you now and again in spite of yourself – then I say that this alone is able to sanctify you. Your life may be said to be hard and laborious, a life of suffering and penitence, so that you are having purgatory in this world, which will deliver you in the next, or at any rate greatly lessen the suffering. This is why I dare not ask God deliverance for all eternity by praising His mercifulness. So I can only ask Him for obedience, and the total submission in your suffering state. It is God's mercy that you are not unduly sensitive at the thought of death. Endure your inward indifferences and boredom like your other bodily ills. God asks nothing else of you. A single *Fiat!* a day can and must bring about your salvation and even your perfection. All that books and directors could tell you is reduced to that single word *Fiat!*, always and for all things, but especially with regard to the penitent and suffering life in which it has pleased Divine Providence to place you. Toby in his blindness, Job on his dung-heap, and so many other saints, both men and women, nailed to their bed of suffering, did no more. It is true that they did it with fewer faults, more perfectly and with greater love.

LETTER 63

1. We never take full advantage, or to the fullest extent, of the good advice given to us, whether it be in writing or by word of mouth. Nevertheless, if it only serves to humiliate without discouraging us or our will to do better. That is already a great deal. Let us live in hope and in total abandonment to God and to all the decisions of his Divine Providence, whose secret ways are a great mystery to us, which we must adore without wanting to discover them in advance.

2. Worldly matters influence us according to how we see them and how closely they affect us. And so I am in no way surprised by what you tell me about your present predicament. Oh what great treasure of merit, grace, peace

and tranquillity total resignation brings! That is why I have preached self-abandonment to you so often, and continue to preach it to you, wishing you to be serene and happy as a saint. But this will come with God's help, little by little.

3. God continues to leave my sick parent in the same state in order to test and convert all his family. If they draw this reward as I have every reason to hope they will, O what a happy accident, worth more than all the wealth in the world!

4. I have just lost my best and closest friend, whom most I have loved and admired and on whom I could count. God so willed it: may His holy will be done.

5. God be blest for and in everything, and for knowing so well how to make use of everything to sanctify one another. About this Archbishop de Cambrai has well said that God often uses one diamond to polish another.

6. Hail and rain have made havoc in many provinces, as in yours. God mercifully allows us to draw profit by all these scourges that come from on high for our sins. A simple and sincere *Fiat!* is worth more than all the abandonment one could wish for, because it is a treasure for eternity. Once we are filled with these high hopes we find ourselves much less susceptible to the misfortunes of this short and miserable life.

7. By thinking about death, we succeed gradually in anticipating it calmly. The incomparable Father Bourdaloue has truly said of this that the thought of death is indeed sad, but by dint of looking upon it as salvation, in

the end it becomes agreeable. And it is reported that a great
Jesuit cardinal said that in that last hour he had never
imagined it was so sweet to die.

8. One sometimes hears: "But I have no support or
   teachings to encourage me." A reason for sacrifice,
Fiat! Fiat! All the most edifying teachings are not worth
what one gains by a simple *Fiat!* during deprivation of all
outward support. The highway to all perfection is confined
to these words of the Our Father only: *Fiat voluntas tua*
etc. You have but to say them with your lips, and even
more with your heart, as best you can, and believe that
with this inward disposition alone nothing will or can fail
you. From that learn to find rest even in all difficulties and
troubles, because everything turns to good when God
wishes it to, and we wish it because God wishes or allows
it. Afflictions and the cross are such great mercies that
wicked people usually only save themselves through them,
and good people only become perfect in the same way.

9. God readily provides everything, and He supplies it
   more readily when we wish only for Him and wait for
everything from Him alone. It is in order to bring us step
by step, and by a fortunate need, to this happy and
desirable disposition, that He often deprives us of all
human support and comfort, just as He drops bitterness
into worldly pleasures to disgust and detach worldly souls
whom He wishes to save . Blessed affliction! Blessed
hardship! When we see clearly that they come more from
God's bounty than His justice, for this is how we must
see them.

Also available in Fount Paperbacks

Silent Music
WILLIAM JOHNSTON

Silent Music is a brilliant synthesis which joins traditional religious insights with the discoveries of modern science to provide a complete picture of mysticism – its techniques and stages, its mental and physical aspects, its dangers, and its consequences.

The Inner Eye of Love
WILLIAM JOHNSTON

'This is a lucid comparison and exposition of eastern and western mysticism, from Zen to the Cloud of Unknowing, which can do nothing but good all round.'

Gerald Priestland, The Universe

The Mirror Mind
WILLIAM JOHNSTON

'William Johnston continues his first-hand studies of Zen meditation and Christian prayer . . . At his disposal he has had a twofold large and demanding literature. His use of it can be startlingly luminous.'

Bernard Lonergan

The Varieties of Religious Experience
WILLIAM JAMES

'A classic of psychological study. . . fresh and stimulating . . . this book is a book to prize.'

The Psychologist

The Religious Experience of Mankind
NINIAN SMART

'Professor Smart's patient, clear and dispassionate exposition makes him a tireless and faithful guide.'

Evening News

Also available in Fount Paperbacks

Poustinia
CATHERINE DE HUECK DOHERTY

'This is not a book, it is a stream of life.'
Father Edward J. Farrell

Molchanie: The Silence of God
CATHERINE DE HUECK DOHERTY

'A deeply reflective and imaginative book, in which the author uses the poetic language of the mystic to describe her encounters with God in the uncreated silence of the Godhead.'
Catholic Herald

Return to the Centre
BEDE GRIFFITHS

' . . . his mind and pen move easily . . . The whole, beautifully written, is a modern classic, leading the reader to the foundations of the spiritual life.'
The Times

The Golden String
BEDE GRIFFITHS

'A book of Christian and Catholic autobiography that stands altogether apart from most books for the revelation it contains . . . told in language of classical and mystical beauty.'
Michael de la Bedoyere, Catholic Herald

The Marriage of East and West
BEDE GRIFFITHS

This sequel to *The Golden String* offers hope for the future, based on the consciousness of the holy in the midst of each being and of the presence of God in man and nature.

Also available in Fount Paperbacks

Jesus – The Man Who Lives
MALCOLM MUGGERIDGE

'This book is excellently produced and beautifully illustrated
. . . it bears witness to Malcolm Muggeridge's deep convictions,
his devotion to the person of Jesus.'
Mervyn Stockwood, Church of England Newspaper

Jesus Rediscovered
MALCOLM MUGGERIDGE

'. . . one of the most beautifully written, perverse, infuriating,
enjoyable and moving books of the year.'
David Edwards, Church Times

Mister Jones, Meet the Master
PETER MARSHALL

'Here is a book of sermons like nothing else on earth . . .
forthright, easily understood and intensely human . . .'
Hector Harrison, NSW Presbyterian

Fount Paperbacks

Fount is one of the leading paperback publishers of religious books and below are some of its recent titles.

- [ ] THE WAY OF THE CROSS Richard Holloway £1.95
- [ ] LIKE WIND ON THE GRASSES Rita Snowden £1.95
- [ ] AN INTRODUCTION TO MARITAL PROBLEMS Jack Dominian £2.50
- [ ] I AM WITH YOU John Woolley £2.95
- [ ] NOW AND FOR EVER Anne Townsend £1.95
- [ ] THE PERFECTION OF LOVE Tony Castle £2.95
- [ ] A PROPHETIC PEOPLE Clifford Hill £2.95
- [ ] THOMAS MORE Richard Marius £7.95
- [ ] WALKING IN THE LIGHT David Winter £1.95
- [ ] HALF WAY Jim Thompson £2.50
- [ ] THE HEART OF THE BIBLE George Appleton £4.95
- [ ] I BELIEVE Trevor Huddleston £1.75
- [ ] PRESENT CONCERNS C. S. Lewis £1.95
- [ ] PSALMS OF PRAISE Frances Hogan £2.50
- [ ] MOTHER TERESA: CONTEMPLATIVE IN THE HEART OF THE WORLD Angelo Devananda £2.50
- [ ] IN THE HURRICANE Adrian Hastings £2.50

All Fount paperbacks are available at your bookshop or newsagent, or they can be ordered by post from Fount Paperbacks, Cash Sales Department, G.P.O. Box 29, Douglas, Isle of Man, British Isles. Please send purchase price plus 15p per book, maximum postage £3. Customers outside the UK send purchase price, plus 15p per book. Cheque, postal order or money order. No currency.

NAME (Block letters)_____

ADDRESS_____

_____

While every effort is made to keep prices low, it is sometimes necessary to increase them at short notice. Fount Paperbacks reserve the right to show new retail prices on covers which may differ from those previously advertised in the text or elsewhere.